WRITTEN BY TOM ADAMS

ILLUSTRATED BY
DANIELA MARTÍN DEL CAMPO

 Penguin Random House

Written by Tom Adams
Illustrated by Daniela Martín del Campo

Project Editor Abi Maxwell
Project Art Editor Bettina Myklebust Stovne
Managing Art Editor Diane Peyton Jones
Production Editor Gillian Reid
Production Controller Leanne Burke
Publisher James Mitchem
Managing Art Editor Mabel Chan

First published in Great Britain in 2026 by
Dorling Kindersley Limited
20 Vauxhall Bridge Road,
London SW1V 2SA

The authorised representative in the EEA is
Dorling Kindersley Verlag GmbH. Arnulfstr. 124,
80636 Munich, Germany

Text copyright © Tom Adams 2026
Illustration copyright © Daniela Martín del Campo 2026
Copyright © 2026 Dorling Kindersley Limited
A Penguin Random House Company
10 9 8 7 6 5 4 3 2 1
001–351407–April/2026

All rights reserved.
No part of this publication may be reproduced, stored in or introduced into a retrieval system, or transmitted, in any form, or by any means (electronic, mechanical, photocopying, recording, or otherwise), without the prior written permission of the copyright owner.
DK values and supports copyright. Thank you for respecting intellectual property laws by not reproducing, scanning or distributing any part of this publication by any means without permission. By purchasing an authorised edition, you are supporting writers and artists and enabling DK to continue to publish books that inform and inspire readers. No part of this publication may be used or reproduced in any manner for the purpose of training artificial intelligence technologies or systems.
In accordance with Article 4(3) of the DSM Directive 2019/790, DK expressly reserves this work from the text and data mining exception.

A CIP catalogue record for this book
is available from the British Library.
ISBN: 978-0-2417-6337-7

Printed and bound in China

www.dk.com

CONTENTS

NATURE AND HISTORY

- 06 Peking man
- 08 Unfinished explorations
- 10 The Copper Scroll Treasure
- 12 Extinct is forever
- 14 Ancient trees

PLACES

- 16 Port Royal
- 18 Great leaders, lost forever
- 20 Queens of the ancients
- 22 The lost Wonders
- 24 The Amber Room
- 26 Lost in the desert

PEOPLE

- 28 D. B. Cooper
- 30 The President's brain is missing
- 32 Kings, playwrights, and revolutionaries
- 34 The Roman Ninth Legion
- 36 Lost at sea

ART

- 38 Nazi-looted art
- 40 Daleks and Disney
- 42 Writers' block
- 44 Stolen!
- 46 The Bayeux Tapestry
- 48 Jewels and jewellery

KNOWLEDGE

- 50 Ancient wisdom
- 52 Lincoln's lost speech
- 54 Lost libraries
- 56 The original renaissance man
- 58 Lost games

TREASURE

- 60 Treasure!
- 62 Gold rush
- 64 Tucker's cross
- 66 Going for gold
- 68 The Jules Rimet trophy
- 70 Sporting losses
- 72 Royal treasures
- 74 Crowns missing their jewels
- 76 Ancient Chinese artefacts
- 78 Hidden gems

TECH AND INNOVATION

- 80 Swordquest!
- 82 Ancient technology, gone missing
- 84 Probes and orbiters
- 86 Not just any old rock
- 88 Bombs away
- 90 Missing bitcoin

- 92 Glossary
- 94 index
- 96 Acknowledgements

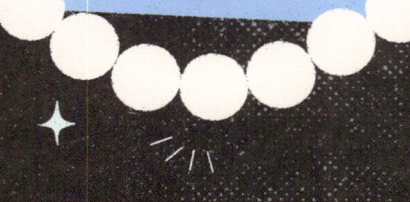

INTRODUCTION

Have you ever lost anything? Your pocket money? The TV remote? Socks? It happens all the time. It's no surprise then that across the world, many extraordinary things have gone missing over the centuries. Time and time again, the most treasured possessions seem to vanish. And it's not just objects... You name it, someone's lost it!

Across the pages of this book, you'll discover how people, great artworks, royal jewels, ancient tombs, pirate treasure, pieces of our natural world, religious artefacts, and even technology and space kit have all gone missing.

But being "lost" can mean a number of things. Here you'll learn of languages that have died out, animals that have been hunted to extinction, and objects destroyed through greed, or simply ignorance. All of them are now lost to humankind.

Other lost objects still survive – they just need finding. However, you won't come across them down the back of a sofa (ahh, the remote!) or in the laundry basket (although the football World Cup trophy did spend years hidden under someone's bed). No, these lost treasures might be locked away in a private collection away from prying eyes, or perhaps waiting for someone like you to discover them at the bottom of the ocean.

What did they find?

It was a collection of bones from an ancient species of human that lived about half a million years ago. They appeared to be from a species never before discovered. Named Peking Man, the people were found to be from the *Homo erectus* family – a much earlier family than the humans of today.

Peking Man was slightly shorter than us, with long arms. Importantly, the skulls revealed these people had big brains, and the axes found alongside the bones suggested they could make and use tools, and create fire, something only more advanced species can do.

The discovery had the potential to redefine our own history, but it would take many years of studying the bones to fully understand them.

But all work has stopped on the Peking Man finds. Why? Because the bones have vanished!

1921

The cave containing the fossilized bones was found roughly 50 km (30 miles) outside of Beijing.

PEKING MAN
ANCIENT FOSSILS LOST IN THE FOG OF WAR.

In the 1920s, a team of archaeologists excavating a cave close to Beijing, China, discovered a treasure trove of fossilized bones. The locals called the site "Dragon Bone Hill" after the fossils of ancient animals found there previously, but these archaeologists had stumbled upon something far more interesting.

The fossilized skull of Peking man revealed they had large brains and wide noses.

1941

1947

What happened?

In 1941, with China and its neighbour, Japan, at war, archaeologists were concerned that these precious fossils might be damaged if Beijing was bombed. A plan was made to smuggle them out of Beijing, for safekeeping.

The bones were packed into two wooden crates and then shipped across China to a US military base on the coast. However, Japan invaded China, and as World War Two ended, China descended into civil war. Keeping tabs on the fossils was impossible and the bones have been missing ever since.

Where could they be?

The biggest clue comes from a US Marine who was stationed at that US military base on the coast in 1947. Under fire, he dug himself a shelter close to the camp and uncovered a crate filled with bones. More interested in staying alive than investigating fossils, he left the box where he found it. The story only came to light about 60 years later!

Today, a huge warehouse sits where the base once stood. The chest of bones may still be there, but under feet of tarmac. So, for now, the bones remain lost.

NATURE AND HISTORY

This altimeter, which measures the altitude (height) of an object, was found on the body of George Mallory in 1999.

UNFINISHED EXPLORATIONS

TOP OF THE WORLD

In 1953, Tenzing Norgay and Edmund Hillary became famous for being the first climbers to scale Mount Everest, the tallest peak in the world. But in 1924, nearly 30 years earlier, two other climbers had attempted the peak: George Mallory and Andrew "Sandy" Irvine.

Mount Everest is 8,848 m (29,031 ft) tall, and still growing!

Sadly, Mallory and Irvine perished in the attempt, and their bodies weren't recovered for decades. But did they reach the summit? Did they lose their lives on their way up the mountain, or on their way down? Nobody else accompanied them on their attempt to make history, so surely it's impossible to know. Except...

The pair carried with them a small camera known as a Vest Pocket Kodak, or VPK. This was a simple camera that took photographs on film, different to the digital cameras of today. Had the two mountaineers reached the summit, surely they would have taken a celebratory photo of themselves on top of the world.

Irvine (left) and Mallory (right), before their 1924 summit attempt.

If this camera could be found, perhaps it might reveal if they were the first up Everest or not.

In 1999, Mallory's body was found, frozen in the ice. No camera was found though. In 2024, hikers discovered one of Irvine's boots – with his foot still inside! But the rest of his body, and the all-important camera, are still missing.

The VPK was one of the first pocket-sized cameras, making it popular with soldiers during the First World War.

> LOST...
> BEFORE MAKING IT
> BACK TO BASE.

AROUND THE WORLD

Amelia Earhart was a fearless aviator. She was the first woman to fly solo across the Atlantic Ocean, and she set many other aviation firsts. On 1 June 1937, she took off from Florida in the US, with the aim of becoming the first female pilot to circumnavigate the world by plane.

Alongside Amelia was her navigator, Fred Noonan. They headed to South America first, then flew across the Atlantic to Africa, then to India, and Southeast Asia. By late June, they reached Lae in New Guinea – finally on the home straight.

On the morning of 2 July, Earhart and Noonan left Lae for Howland Island, a pinprick of land in the Pacific Ocean. During the 4,200 km (2,600 mile) journey, the pair made contact with the US Coast Guard boat *Itasca*, which was patrolling the area. It was the last contact Earhart and Noonan ever made. As far as we know, they never reached Howland Island.

A huge search effort followed, but the plane and the pair on board were never found. On 19 July 1937, Earhart and Noonan were officially declared lost at sea.

Many theories as to what happened to them have sprung up since the disappearance. Perhaps the pair lost their bearings and ran out of fuel? Or did they find land only to be eaten by coconut crabs? With no hard evidence of either Earhart or Noonan ever found, and no sign of the plane, what happened on that fateful flight to Howland Island remains a mystery.

Amelia flew in her twin-engine Lockheed 10E Electra plane.

Nobody knows what happened to Earhart and Noonan, only that they never arrived at their destination of Howland Island.

Astonishing find

Made of papyrus and animal skin, these scrolls were Jewish manuscripts dated from the 3rd century BCE to the 2nd century CE containing, among other things, writings from the Old Testament of the Bible. For archaeologists and religious academics, it was one of the most exciting finds in modern times.

But there was another scroll, made from metal rather than animal skin. Three wafer-thin sheets of copper were discovered on a shelf carved into one of the caves. Unfurling them revealed Hebrew text engraved into the metal.

Almost 15,000 scrolls and scroll fragments have been found around the caves.

THE COPPER SCROLL TREASURE

TREASURE CAN TAKE MANY FORMS.

In 1947, in a series of caves on the shores of the Dead Sea, a remarkable discovery was made: a collection of ancient scrolls, rolled up in several pottery jars.

Long-lost treasure

The papyrus scrolls contained writings from the Bible, hymns and prayers, and details about the beliefs and practices of the people who left the manuscripts. However, the copper scroll told of something quite different: a collection of treasures hidden at 64 sites across Israel.

Those treasures included more than 100 tonnes (110 tons) of gold and silver worth millions of pounds today. Except, with clues such as "in the salt pit that is under the steps", "41 talents of silver in the cave of the old washer's chamber", and "on the third terrace: 65 ingots of gold", the descriptions of the hiding places are all so vague that it's impossible to know where to start looking. Since the copper scroll was deciphered, around 70 years ago, a grand total of none of the treasures have been found!

Unable to fully unfurl the corroded metal, scientists cut the scroll into 23 sections.

NATURE AND HISTORY

EXTINCT IS FOREVER

THE DODO

The dodo was a flightless bird that was only found on the island of Mauritius, in the Indian Ocean. It survived there for thousands of years, until humans arrived in the 16th century. A century later, not a single dodo remained.

It's hard to know what the dodo looked like. From written descriptions and the few bones that remain, they are thought to have been around 1 m (3 ft) tall, with grey feathers, a bald head, and a large black, yellow, and green beak. They waddled around the island like oversized turkeys.

Dodos had never encountered humans before, so when Dutch sailors landed on Mauritius in 1598, the birds weren't scared.

Because they couldn't fly and didn't run away when approached, they were easy to hunt. The sailors also brought other animals onto the island, including dogs, pigs, and cats. These animals either hunted the dodos, or ate things on the island that the dodos would normally eat. Many of the birds went hungry and starved.

By the early 17th century, every dodo was gone. And because they were not found on any other island, that was the end of the species, forever. The loss of the dodo reveals just what harm we humans can do if we're not careful.

Dodo bones are our only way of knowing what they looked like, as they became extinct before cameras were invented.

SO MANY SPECIES HAVE BEEN LOST DUE TO HUMAN ACTIONS. HERE ARE A COUPLE.

None of the lions currently in zoos are pure Barbary, but descendants of the species.

THE BARBARY LiON

The Barbary lion once roamed the deserts and mountains of North Africa. Living in colder climates than their sub-Saharan cousins, they had shaggier manes and thicker coats to keep them warm.

They were grand beasts, and much admired. During the time of the Roman Empire, thousands of these lions were captured and shipped to Rome to fight gladiators in the Colosseum. Later, they were taken for zoos or kept as pets by dignitaries and royal families across Europe.

As the human population of North Africa increased, so decreased the areas the lions could live undisturbed. The lions continued to be hunted and their numbers plummeted. The last photograph of a Barbary lion in the wild was taken in 1925. Another was spotted in a forest in Algeria in 1956, but after that? Nothing. The Barbary lion was gone.

While the Barbary lion is lost to the wild, new research suggests that genes from these lions still exist in some animals in zoos across the world. With the help of science, the Barbary lion may just make it back into the wild one day.

NATURE AND HISTORY

ANCIENT TREES

EXTRAORDINARY LIVING THINGS, FELLED BY HUMANS.

There are said to be more than three trillion trees on Earth. With more than eight billion people in the world, that's around four hundred trees for every person. You'd think if one or two get cut down, it wouldn't matter. But it does!

Prometheus

Bristlecone pines are thought to be the oldest living trees, able to survive for thousands of years.

In 1964 a geography student was studying the bristlecones of Wheeler Peak in New Mexico in the US. Here, he came across a particularly ancient tree, one so well known the locals had even given it a name – Prometheus.

You can tell a tree's age from the rings throughout its trunk, and there are ways of counting these without harming the tree. However, this student cut Prometheus down to discover its age.

So how old was this tree? Counting its rings revealed Prometheus to be around 4,900 years old, at the time the oldest tree ever discovered and perhaps the oldest known living thing.

Today, the remains of the tree can still be found in Wheeler Peak, a reminder that perhaps there are limits as to how far we should go to satisfy our own curiosity.

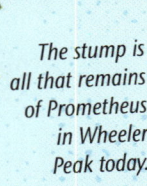

The stump is all that remains of Prometheus in Wheeler Peak today.

Sycamore Gap Tree

Hadrian's Wall runs across the very north of England. Alongside a section of the crumbling wall, a sycamore tree recently stood. The tree was more than 150 years old and a local landmark, sitting in a dip known as Sycamore Gap. It was a significant site for thousands of visitors.

Then, in September 2023, locals woke to discover the tree had been felled overnight. Police were called in to investigate and in time two men were arrested for criminal damage. But putting people in prison for destroying the sycamore doesn't bring the tree back, and many were deeply upset by the loss.

In the meantime, new shoots have grown from the stump that remains in the ground. Perhaps in 150 years' time, one of these shoots will have developed into a tree that is loved as much as the original.

The valley now stands empty, the space between the hills a reminder of the lost tree.

The Tree of Ténéré

300 years ago, deep in the Sahara Desert, a grove of acacia trees once stood. But as the climate grew more severe, the acacias began to die, leaving just one tree. The most isolated tree in the world.

It provided the only shade for 400 km (250 miles) in any direction. Its roots had to dig down some 30 m (100 ft) through the desert to reach water. It seemed like a miracle: life in the harshest of all environments. And the nomads that came across the tree on their travels vowed never to harm it.

Then, in 1973, someone driving a truck through the desert hit the tree, damaging the trunk and ultimately killing it. The trunk was placed in a dedicated shrine in the Niger National Museum. And today, a simple metal sculpture stands where the tree once stood.

Out in the empty desert, the solitary metal sculpture acts as a shrine.

PLACES

PORT ROYAL

A WARNING FROM GOD?

Known as "the wickedest city on Earth" in the 17th century, Port Royal on the Caribbean island of Jamaica was home to pirates, privateers, and a host of other vagabonds. They were all looking to make a fortune from the nearby trade in sugar and enslaved people.

Because of its location, Port Royal was a strategic port for European nations wanting to expand into the Americas. Spain ran the port for nearly 150 years until the English drove them out in 1655. By the late 17th century it was one of the most important trading ports in the western hemisphere.

Lawless land

Port Royal was a place of opportunity, but with that came lawlessness, and there was an "anything goes" attitude on the island. You could make a fortune one day and lose it the next.

Once the English took control, the new governor drafted in a terrifying bunch of pirates and privateers to protect the island from the Spanish. The notorious pirate Henry Morgan was made Lieutenant Governor of the island – when the person in charge is a pirate, you know rules are going to be broken! These swashbucklers did what pirates do, raiding the Spanish ports in the Americas and taking whatever they could. Then on 7 June 1692, a massive earthquake hit the island.

Underwater remains

Much of Port Royal was built on sand, and as the earthquake struck, a lot of the port simply disappeared, sucked below ground. A huge tsunami followed, which wiped away even more of the city. Two-thirds of Port Royal just vanished. Thousands of lives were lost.

Today, Port Royal is a small fishing village, but parts of the old city are perfectly preserved underwater. An amazing find here even hints at the time the earthquake hit the port. A pocket watch was found among the city's remains. It stopped at 11:43 am, suggesting this was the exact time the owner of the watch slipped below the waves.

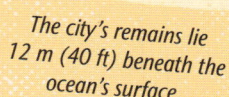

The city's remains lie 12 m (40 ft) beneath the ocean's surface.

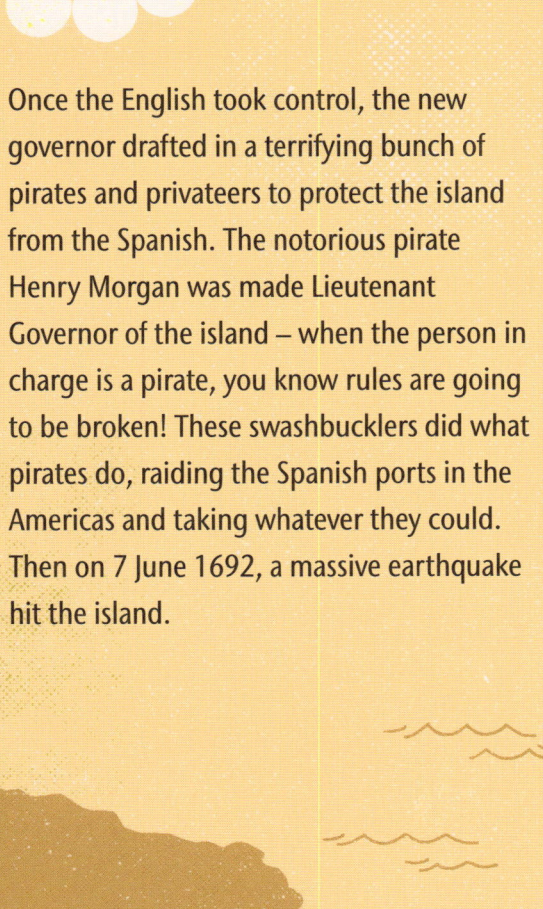

The earthquake had a magnitude of 7.5 on the Richter scale.

PLACES

GREAT LEADERS, LOST FOREVER

WHERE ARE THESE FINAL RESTING PLACES?

Genghis Khan's grave

Genghis Khan ruled Mongolia, a vast country east of Europe, in the early 13th century. His dying wish was to have a hidden burial site.

But how do you ensure your burial place remains secret? One legend claims that the 2,000 enslaved people that buried Khan were then slaughtered by the soldiers sent to watch over them. Those soldiers were then slaughtered, too! Others claim that a thousand horses trampled over the grave site, so that no-one could tell the earth had been freshly dug.

Today, researchers believe Khan is buried somewhere in the Burkhan Khaldun mountain, but many Mongolians would prefer the site of their fabled leader to stay hidden, just as he wanted.

Alexander the Great's tomb

The location of the tomb of Alexander the Great, the ancient Macedonian king, has left archaeologists and historians frustrated for years.

Alexander died in 323 BCE at the age of 32. Once he was gone, his friends and supporters fought for control of his empire, which was torn apart by civil war for decades.

But they weren't only fighting for land. Whoever held Alexander's body would be seen as the legitimate heir to his empire.

Some historians even suggest that Alexander's body ended up in St Mark's Basilica, in Venice.

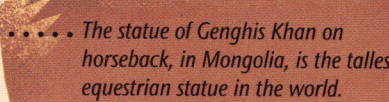
The statue of Genghis Khan on horseback, in Mongolia, is the tallest equestrian statue in the world.

How do you lose the body of a great leader? It's easier than you might think. Here are three very different rulers whose tombs are all lost, each for very different reasons.

Alexander died in Babylon, a city in what is now Iraq. As his body was being transported back to his homeland, Macedonia, it was stolen by Ptolomy, one of Alexander's most trusted generals, and taken to Memphis, in Egypt.

But the body ended up in Alexandria in Egypt, where we know Julius Caesar paid his respects in 48 BCE. It was still there 263 years later when another Roman emperor, Caracalla, visited.

Archaeologists have since scoured Alexandria for a tomb but found nothing. Is it still there? Or did it move again? The mystery remains unsolved.

Sarcophagus of Menkaure

Menkaure was an ancient king who ruled Egypt more than 4,000 years ago, laid to rest in one of the pyramids of Giza.

In 1837, British explorer Howard Vyse broke into the burial chamber and discovered a chipped, brown-and-blue basalt sarcophagus – the great stone container built to hold the pharaoh's body.

Although Menkaure's body had already been taken by grave robbers, Vyse arranged for the casket to be shipped to Britain. Unfortunately, the vessel sank in a storm somewhere off the coast of Spain. Despite many teams hunting for the lost ship, it has never been found. The sarcophagus is down there somewhere. But where?

Menkaure's pyramid stands on the Giza plateau, outside of Cairo in Egypt.

PLACES

Nefertiti's burial site

Nefertiti was Queen of Egypt more than 3,000 years ago. She was the wife of the pharaoh Akhenaten, possibly even ruling after his death, and stepmother to Tutankhamun. She was at the heart of a fascinating period of Egyptian history.

But where is she buried? Archaeologists have searched for years. The Valley of the Kings, an ancient burial ground in Luxor where rulers of Egypt were laid to rest over the centuries, is a possibility. The tombs of great pharaohs, including Tutankhamun, are all there.

Recently, researchers thought they had found clues that led to a hidden chamber in Tutankhamun's tomb that might have contained her mummy. But so far, no tomb has been found, and the search for her remains continues.

Cleopatra's tomb

Cleopatra was queen of Egypt from 51 BCE to 30 BCE. When her partner, the Roman general Mark Anthony, died, she decided she didn't want to live without him. She let a poisonous snake bite her.

Almost immediately, her burial site was a mystery. Augustus, Mark Anthony's opponent in battle, searched for it in vain. Hundreds of years later, French dictator Napoleon Bonaparte organized a scientific expedition to Egypt, where another unsuccessful search for the tomb was also carried out.

Isis was a favourite goddess of Cleopatra's, making the Taposiris Magna a likely burial place for the Egyptian queen.

The tomb of Tutankhamun is a suspected burial site for his stepmother, Nefertiti.

QUEENS OF THE ANCIENTS

THREE POWERFUL WOMEN... LOST TO HISTORY.

So where might Cleopatra be? One theory is the port of Alexandria, Egypt's capital in Cleopatra's day. Unfortunately, much of ancient Alexandria is now underwater, making searching for the tomb tricky!

Another potential site is at Taposiris Magna, a temple complex close to Alexandria. Inside a temple dedicated to the Egyptian goddess of magic and wisdom, Isis, are hidden passages and chambers carved with images of Cleopatra. As of yet, there is no body. Perhaps there are more secret spaces to be found here…

Boudicca's grave

A fierce warrior queen and leader of the Iceni, a tribe of ancient Britons, Boudicca rebelled against the Roman invaders who ruled her country in 60 BCE. The Romans ultimately defeated her army at the Battle of Watling Street. Although she survived the battle itself, her death remains a mystery.

And the location of her grave? Nobody knows, although that hasn't stopped some bizarre theories emerging. Is she buried under London's Kings Cross railway station? Or Hampstead Heath, where there's even a mound known as "Boudicca's Grave"?

However, perhaps her grave has already been found. In 1879 in Birdlip in Gloucestershire, archaeologists discovered a stash of ancient treasures, alongside a female skeleton. Could this be the Queen of the Iceni?

A host of ancient objects, such as bowls, jewellery, and this mirror, were discovered in Birdlip in 1879.

Nothing screams "mystery" quite like a vanishing. The remains of these three great women are all lost in the mists of time, adding a healthy dose of intrigue to their legacy.

PLACES ?

THE LOST WONDERS

NOT A TRACE REMAINS OF SOME OF THE SEVEN WONDERS.

Ancient authors wrote of seven incredible feats of human achievement, structures that redefined what was believed possible. They became known as the Seven Wonders of the World. One of these Wonders, the Great Pyramid at Giza, still stands, and evidence remains of three more: the Mausoleum of Halicarnassus, the Temple of Artemis, and the Lighthouse of Alexandria. Of the final three though, no solid trace exists.

The Hanging Gardens of Babylon

Babylon was said to be the most spectacular city on Earth. Today, its ruins are found 80 km (50 miles) from Baghdad in Iraq. And while there have been some amazing archaeological finds here, there's been no sign of the Gardens.

They were said to have been built by King Nebuchadnezzar in around 600 BCE. If they did exist, a rich, verdant garden in the heat of the Babylonian sun would have been a wonder of the age. We know Nebuchadnezzar built many structures across Babylon as he kept detailed written records of his achievements. But he never mentions gardens, and if they did exist, we have little evidence as to what they really looked like.

The Colossus of Rhodes

According to ancient authors, a huge bronze statue of the ancient Greek sun god, Helios, once stood on the island of Rhodes. It was said to be over 30 m (98 ft) tall, and was known as the Colossus.

In 226 BCE, just 54 years after the statue was erected, an earthquake hit Rhodes and destroyed it. It was never rebuilt. But where did it stand? And what did it look like?

No remains have ever been found, so it's unclear where the Colossus stood. Engravings made long after its disappearance show it straddling the harbour, but building there would have required the waterfront to close for months, perhaps years. Would an island so dependent upon ships for supplies and trade do such a thing?

A more likely location is a high point in the island's capital where the statue could have been seen for miles around. Here, archaeologists have uncovered evidence of a temple dedicated to Helios. Was there a statue there, too?

The Statue of Zeus

In a temple at Olympia, on the Peloponnese peninsula in Greece, a gold and ivory statue of Zeus once stood more than 12 m (39 ft) tall. It was a masterpiece created by one of the ancient world's most revered sculptors, Phideas. For the Greeks, Zeus was king of the gods, and while the workshop of Phideas still exists today, the statue itself is long gone.

Quite what happened to it, though, is a mystery. In 391 CE, the Roman emperor Theodosius, a Christian, banned gods worshipped by other religions. The temple at Olympia was closed down. Some believe the statue may have survived the ban though, being moved to Constantinople (modern-day Istanbul). Here it is thought that the statue was lost in a fire.

THE AMBER ROOM

A STUNNING TREASURE LOST IN THE CHAOS OF WAR.

Amber is ancient tree resin that, over thousands of years, turns into a hard, glass-like substance. The Amber Room, so-called because it was lined with the golden resin, was so beautiful that it was once dubbed the Eighth Wonder of the World.

In 1701 Frederick I, king of the German state of Prussia, called for a room to be constructed that was lined with golden slivers of amber for his palace in Berlin. No-one had ever used amber like this before, and the result was a room like no other.

When the Russian tsar, Peter the Great, saw the room in 1716, he fell so in love with it that he was given it as a gift! The whole room was packed into boxes, and shipped to St Petersburg in Russia.

For more than 200 years, the Amber Room continued to dazzle. Then, during the Second World War, Hitler wanted to reclaim the Amber Room and bring it back to Germany. When the Nazis pushed into Russia, the Russians knew they had to protect the room somehow.

But over the centuries, the amber had become fragile and removing the panels would likely cause damage. Could the treasure be hidden instead? Perhaps.

BERLIN

ST PETERSBURG

KÖNIGSBERG

Today, there is another Amber Room, copied from a series of black-and-white photos that were taken of the original room just before war broke out. It took over 20 years to recreate, but it now sits in Catherine Palace in St Petersburg.

The amber was too brittle to disassemble and pack away, so the Russians covered the room up with wallpaper instead. Would it fool the Nazis? Not for a minute!

They found the room and transported it to the German city of Königsberg (today known as Kaliningrad in Russia) and rebuilt it. When Königsberg was bombed late in the war, the order was given to pack the room up again for shipping to Berlin, but here the trail goes cold.

Amber is more commonly used to decorate trinket boxes than whole rooms!

Where is it now?

So what did become of the Amber Room? Some believe it was destroyed in the battle for Königsberg. Others think the Nazis managed to hide the crates in a labyrinth of tunnels under the city.

After the war, the Soviets conducted thorough investigations in and around Königsberg to try and track the treasure down. Bringing the Amber Room back to St Petersburg would have been a great success story for the Russian leadership keen to impress the rest of the world. But despite all efforts, the Amber Room remained lost.

PLACES

Ubar

In the 1930s, European travellers exploring the Arabian Desert were told of an ancient city called Ubar. It's said that thousands of years ago it was a city of treasures, with wonderful gardens and a fort of silver. However, its people shunned their god, so he sent a sandstorm to punish them.

After seven days and seven nights of storms, the city was lost beneath the sand, forever.

As tales of the city spread, explorers came searching for it and the treasures within. In 1948, the ruins of a fort were discovered close to a village called Shis'r. Was this Ubar? It didn't seem ancient enough.

In the 1990s, archaeologists continued the hunt. Taking aerial photos, they spotted ancient camel tracks appearing to converge close to the fort at Shis'r. The archaeologists began digging, and discovered the remains of an older fortress and a city wall thought to be around 2,000 years old.

It sounded promising, until they discovered this city had been destroyed not by a sandstorm, but by a sinkhole in the ground... This wasn't the city they were looking for. And so the search for Ubar and its lost treasures continues.

The ancient remains found at Shis'r may be the closest we ever come to finding the lost city of Ubar.

LOST IN THE DESERT

DESERTS ARE TOUGH PLACES TO SURVIVE, BUT ARE HUMANS TO BLAME HERE?

Palmyra

The city of Palmyra in the Syrian desert was one of the most important artistic centres in the ancient world. In the first century it hosted a meeting of cultures, with ancient Greek, Roman, and Persian influences creating a city like no other.

1,500 years later, the ruins of the city were rediscovered, and the clues found there revealed amazing details. There were temples, a theatre, and a large central high street lined with public monuments and sculptures. An aqueduct provided water, and outside the city walls the citizens buried their dead in elaborate cemeteries.

Then, in the 21st century, sections of this ancient city were bombed by a terrorist group. Parts of a temple complex, the theatre, and the city's monumental entrance, the Great Tetrapylon, were destroyed — a senseless act of violence, and a shocking loss that can never be replaced.

Only parts of the Great Tetrapylon, the original entrance to the ancient city, are left standing today.

Juukan Gorge

In the Pilbara region of Western Australia, Juukan Gorge is the site of rock shelters that have been home to humans for thousands of years. Or at least, they used to be. In 2020, a mining company destroyed them, in a hunt for buried iron ore.

Six years before the destruction, archaeologists found ancient tools, human hair, and thousands of other objects that revealed humans had lived in these caves almost constantly for 45,000 years.

The land was protected First Nation land, a sacred site for the Puutu Kunti Kuruma and Pinikura peoples. However, the mining company received permission from the government to destroy the caves. Now, laws in Western Australia have been changed, in the hope of preventing another tragedy like this.

People have always found ways to survive the harshest of conditions. These three ancient settlements, in deserts across the planet, are proof. Yet all three have vanished, largely due to human behaviour.

The Juukan Gorge was one of the oldest known sites of First Australian settlement.

WANTED

D. B. COOPER

JUMPED INTO THIN AIR.

LAST SEEN:
24 NOVEMBER 1971
OVER WASHINGTON, USA

On 24 November 1971, a man dressed in a smart suit bought a one-way plane ticket for a flight from Portland to Seattle, a journey of a little more than an hour. He gave his name as Dan Cooper. Nothing seemed out of the ordinary.

Once on the plane, Cooper handed the flight attendant a note. He claimed to have a bomb in his briefcase and to prove it, he opened the case to reveal a mass of wires and what appeared to be sticks of dynamite. Cooper demanded that once the plane landed in Seattle, he be given four parachutes and $200,000 (over $1.5 million today) in $20 bills. If the cash failed to appear, he would blow up the plane and everyone on board. Money and parachutes were provided at Seattle, and true to his word, Cooper released the passengers and flight crew – all except for two pilots, a flight engineer, and a flight attendant. These four were to fly him from Seattle to Mexico City.

A leap of faith

Once airborne, he instructed the pilots to lower their altitude and reduce their speed, a tricky manoeuvre in a large passenger jet. Then, somewhere over the small community of Ariel, Washington, Cooper jumped from the plane with his bag of money under his arm and a parachute on his back.

Some wondered if Cooper could have survived the jump. Even flying low and slow, jumping from a passenger jet is a risky stunt to pull off! If he did make it down alive, the terrain around Ariel is rugged and forested. Cooper could have got caught in a tree, or worse. Either he was an expert parachutist who believed he had the skills to survive the jump, or a complete novice who was unaware of the dangers he was facing.

The perfect crime?

After the hijacking, the FBI launched one of the biggest manhunts in history. 800 suspects were identified, and one man, Richard Floyd McCoy, was even arrested for his role in a plane hijacking just five months later. But McCoy didn't match descriptions of Cooper given to police by a number of witnesses. Cooper has never been found, and nobody has ever been charged for the crime.

D. B. Cooper's plane ticket from his fateful flight

In 1980, a young boy found a strange bundle half-buried in the banks of the Columbia River a few miles from Ariel. It contained almost $6,000 in $20 bills. It's the only money from Cooper's $200,000 ever recovered.

PEOPLE

THE PRESIDENT'S BRAIN IS MISSING

WHERE IS JFK'S BRAIN, AND DOES IT HOLD CLUES TO HIS DEATH?

JFK was on the first day of a two-day trip to Dallas when he was killed.

In 1963, US President John F. Kennedy (known as JFK) was shot and killed as he rode in a motorcade through Dallas, Texas.

Three years later, it was discovered that his brain, removed from his body during an autopsy, had gone missing. Why is this important? Because it could provide vital information about the fateful shot that killed him.

On 22 November 1963 JFK was travelling in an open-topped car on a 10-mile journey, waving to a crowd eager to get a glimpse of the charismatic 35th President of the United States. There were more than a dozen cars in the motorcade, carrying local dignitaries, secret service bodyguards, and police. At 12:30 pm, as JFK's car passed a book storage building, shots rang out. The President had been hit by at least two bullets. He was raced to a nearby hospital but was pronounced dead just half an hour later. Cause of death? A gunshot wound to the head.

John F. Kennedy

The FBI investigates

It is widely believed that Lee Harvey Oswald fired at the President from a window on the sixth floor of the book storage building. Oswald never confessed, and died before he could stand trial.

So, was Oswald alone responsible for JFK's death, or was someone else involved?

To try and answer this question, the FBI was tasked with investigating the assassination. Eyewitnesses were quizzed on what they saw, the president's body was examined, and footage filmed by the crowd was pored over for clues.

Three shots were fired at the President from a book storage building along the motorcade route.

Investigators concluded that JFK was shot by the former US Marine, Lee Harvey Oswald, and that he acted alone. But not everyone agrees with the FBI. If the president's brain could be found, investigators could examine the damage, work out the direction in which the bullet that killed the President travelled, and discover once and for all, the truth about JFK's murder.

Today, the book storage building holds a museum dedicated to the assassination.

PEOPLE

KINGS, PLAYWRIGHTS, AND REVOLUTIONARIES

MISSING BODY PARTS – HOW GRUESOME!

These three figures enjoyed the height of fame when alive, yet in death, all had the indignity of having body parts go missing. Is there nothing that can just be left alone?

The Heart of a King

When Louis XIV, the 18th-century King of France, died, he had his heart removed and displayed in a church in Paris. During the French Revolution some 70 years later, revolutionaries, desperate for money, took the heart and sold it! It was bought by the artist Alexandre Pau.

Back in the 18th century, many artists loved the colour known as "mummy brown". It was made by grinding up bits of Egyptian mummy and mixing the powder with water or oils. Louis XIV's old heart was perfect for making mummy brown.

But a little bit of heart was left over. It found its way onto the dinner table of one William Buckland, geologist and palaeontologist, who had set himself the challenge of eating his way through the entire animal kingdom!

At the time of Louis XIV's death, it was customary to remove the organs before burial of the body.

Louis XIV

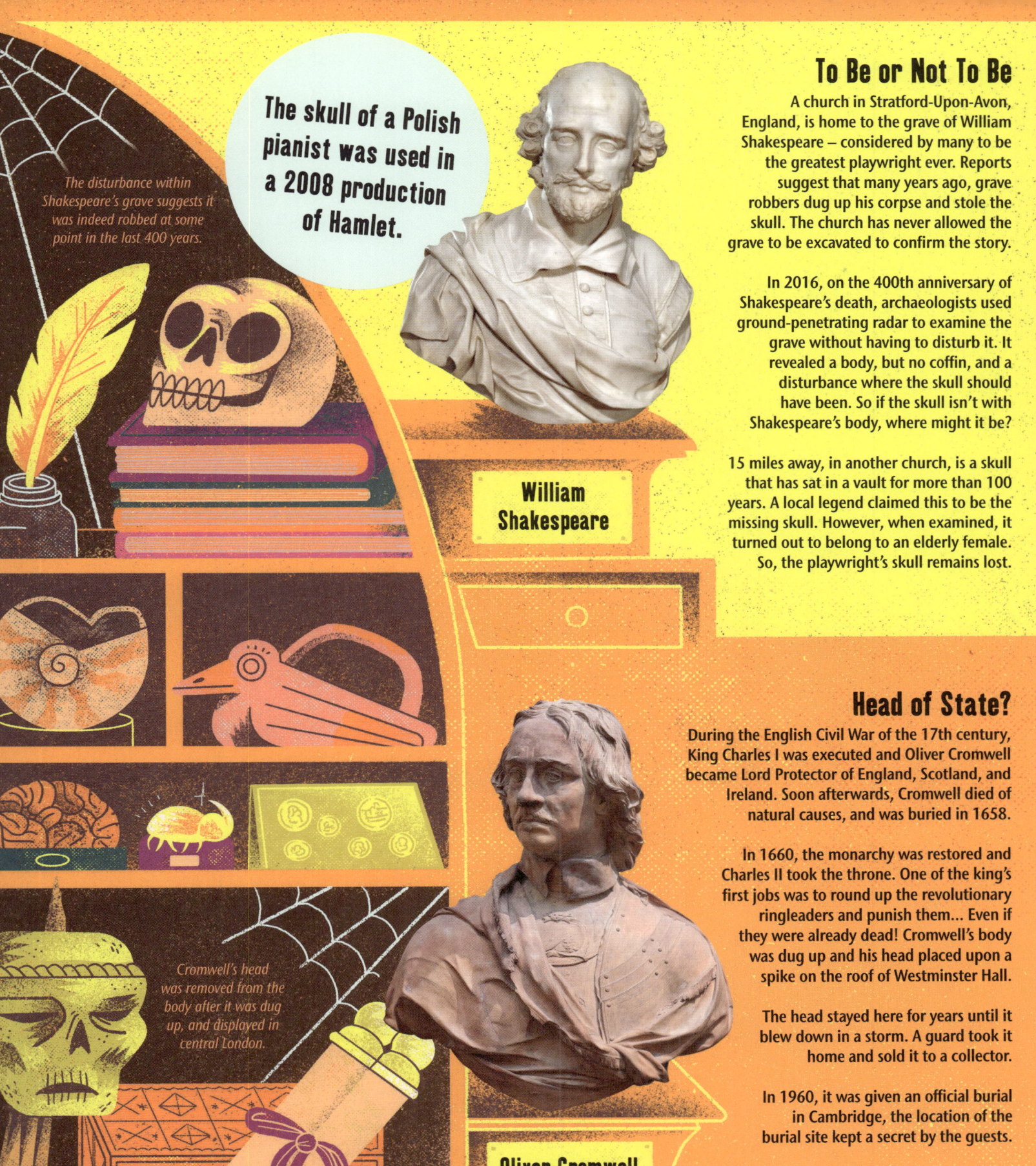

The disturbance within Shakespeare's grave suggests it was indeed robbed at some point in the last 400 years.

The skull of a Polish pianist was used in a 2008 production of Hamlet.

William Shakespeare

Cromwell's head was removed from the body after it was dug up, and displayed in central London.

Oliver Cromwell

To Be or Not To Be

A church in Stratford-Upon-Avon, England, is home to the grave of William Shakespeare — considered by many to be the greatest playwright ever. Reports suggest that many years ago, grave robbers dug up his corpse and stole the skull. The church has never allowed the grave to be excavated to confirm the story.

In 2016, on the 400th anniversary of Shakespeare's death, archaeologists used ground-penetrating radar to examine the grave without having to disturb it. It revealed a body, but no coffin, and a disturbance where the skull should have been. So if the skull isn't with Shakespeare's body, where might it be?

15 miles away, in another church, is a skull that has sat in a vault for more than 100 years. A local legend claimed this to be the missing skull. However, when examined, it turned out to belong to an elderly female. So, the playwright's skull remains lost.

Head of State?

During the English Civil War of the 17th century, King Charles I was executed and Oliver Cromwell became Lord Protector of England, Scotland, and Ireland. Soon afterwards, Cromwell died of natural causes, and was buried in 1658.

In 1660, the monarchy was restored and Charles II took the throne. One of the king's first jobs was to round up the revolutionary ringleaders and punish them... Even if they were already dead! Cromwell's body was dug up and his head placed upon a spike on the roof of Westminster Hall.

The head stayed here for years until it blew down in a storm. A guard took it home and sold it to a collector.

In 1960, it was given an official burial in Cambridge, the location of the burial site kept a secret by the guests.

33

Building a reputation

The Second Legion headed to the south west, the Twentieth and Fourteenth were charged with bringing Wales to order, and the Ninth headed north to force the people there into submission.

When a rebellion stirred in East Anglia, led by Boudicca, Queen of the Iceni, it was the Ninth who were called upon to restore order.

However, it didn't go quite to plan, and the unruly Britons slaughtered hundreds of the Legion. It was a rare defeat.

But soon the Ninth were back in business, trying to quell Celtic tribes in modern-day Scotland. After that, though, their story is difficult to trace.

Julius Caesar was famous for his military strategy, leading the Roman armies to victory.

THE ROMAN NINTH LEGION

STRUCK DOWN IN THEIR PRIME?

Massacred, or just missing?

The last mention of the Ninth is in an inscription on a stone found in York. Dated to 108 CE, it records a fortress being built here and reads "the Emperor Caesar Nerva Trajan Augustus built this gate by the agency of the Ninth Legion Hispania". After that, nothing.

These were Caesar's crack troops. What happened to them?

While there is a chance they may have left Britain for other European trouble spots, many believe they were most likely massacred here, perhaps by Scottish warriors. Yet no trace of such a battle has ever been found and no Roman historian mentions such an encounter.

Until new archaeology finds some evidence of the Ninth, for now, the Legion remains lost.

An inscription of "LEGVIIII" (referring to the Ninth Legion), dated from 108 CE, was discovered in 1854 in York.

The Roman Ninth Legion were said to be 5,000 of Julius Caesar's bravest and fiercest soldiers. So when Rome conquered ancient Britain in 43 CE, the Ninth were one of four legions chosen to lock down the country.

PEOPLE

LOST AT SEA

TWO SHIPS DISAPPEAR OFF THE COAST OF THE US. WAS THE BERMUDA TRIANGLE TO BLAME?

THE USS CYCLOPS

In March 1918 the *USS Cyclops*, one of the biggest ships in the US Navy, vanished without a trace.

The USS Cyclops was never seen again after 1918.

In February, the ship had set sail from Brazil loaded with metal needed for the US war effort. It was heading for Baltimore via Barbados, where it would refuel and resupply. It made it to Barbados, but never reached Baltimore.

No SOS was ever picked up and no wreck has ever been found. The ship and the 306 souls on board just vanished. As one reporter wrote, "she just disappeared as though some gigantic monster of the sea had grabbed her, men and all, and sent her into the depths of the ocean".

Might the Cyclops have been attacked by a German submarine?

After all, America and Germany were at war. It makes sense, but there's no evidence of German vessels in the area.

Some wondered if there were strange goings on in the Bermuda Triangle, a vast stretch of ocean bounded by Bermuda, Miami, and Puerto Rico. For years, people claimed there were mysterious forces at work here.

The triangle also includes the Puerto Rico Trench. At more than 8 km (5 miles) below sea level, it's the deepest part of the Atlantic Ocean. If the Cyclops did go down here, finding it would be tough!

The Bermuda Triangle is an area where ships and planes seem to disappear under mysterious circumstances, despite no scientific evidence of any paranormal activity.

THE CARROLL A. DEERiNG

"Pet parrot only living creature on board derelict craft."

The unmanned Carroll A. Deering ran aground soon after first appearing, undamaged, out on the waves.

So read the headline of the *Washington Herald* on 3 February 1921. *The Carroll A. Deering*, a five-masted schooner, had appeared out of the mist on Diamond Shoals, a treacherous stretch of water, off Cape Hatteras in North Carolina, US. It quickly ran aground.

It had disappeared in late January off the North Carolina coast. Now here it was, in full sail. But when the Coast Guard boarded the ship to investigate, he found nobody on board. Even stranger, everything appeared in order, except that all 12 crew members were missing, along with the lifeboats.

What had made the crew abandon ship? Pirates? Mutiny? The Bermuda Triangle again?

The Carroll A. Deering was the second ship in as many months to disappear. The *SS Hewitt*, steaming from Texas to Portland, Maine, with its cargo of sulphur, had vanished too. No trace of the wreckage was ever found.

Across the two ships, 58 crew members were lost.

So, what was the cause? A message, found in a bottle washed up on the North Carolina coast, suggested pirates or Russian revolutionaries were to blame, but this was discovered to be a hoax. And so, the mystery remains.

ART

NAZI-LOOTED ART

THE NAZIS TOOK WHAT THEY LIKED. MUCH OF IT STILL REMAINS LOST.

When the Nazi Party took control in Germany in 1933, they had a plan to "Nazify" German art, literature, and music. Hitler wanted to show the German people to be strong, powerful, and pure, and to portray other groups as inferior.

The Nazis began to destroy art they didn't like, imprisoning the artists, or forcing them to flee Germany for their own safety. They also collected paintings and sculptures that matched their view of the world. They forced Jewish art collectors to give up pieces, and once war broke out, they took, or looted, other works of art from galleries and museums across Europe.

The Nazis claimed this looting was a way to protect art – keeping valuable pieces out of harm's way in a time of war. No-one was fooled, though. With most of Europe under Nazi control, senior party members were taking famous artworks for themselves.

Portrait of a Man
This piece, painted in the 15th century by Sandro Botticelli (the artist famous for his *Birth of Venus*), once hung in a gallery in Naples. It was stolen in September 1943.

Head of a Faun
This marble face, created by Renaissance hero Michelangelo, was on display in a museum in Florence when it was taken in 1944. Some believe it is now in Russia, but nobody knows exactly where.

The Monuments Men

The Allies were trying to defeat the Nazis on the battlefields, but they also wanted to stop the art looting. In 1943 they formed the "Monuments, Fine Arts, and Archives Section Unit", otherwise known as the Monuments Men. This was a group of art specialists, protecting culturally significant monuments, churches, and art galleries from damage during the war. Along with the Art Looting Investigation Unit, they went on to hunt down specific pieces the Nazis had stolen.

Works still lost

While the Monuments Men did a great job protecting sites and were able to return much art to their owners, there are thought to be hundreds of thousands of items stolen by the Nazis that have still not been returned.

Some of the most famous missing works include:

The Painter On His Way To Work

This self-portrait by Vincent Van Gogh, painted in 1888, hung for many years in a museum in Magdeburg in Germany. It was taken early in the war and hidden in underground tunnels in Stassfurt.

Sappho

A sculpture by Auguste Rodin, *Sappho* belonged to the collector Hans Rudolf Fürstenberg. Hans, who was Jewish, escaped Germany in 1937, after which his sculpture was taken by the Nazis.

ART

DALEKS AND DISNEY

DOCTOR WHO...OR WHERE?

Doctor Who is famous across the world for sending generations of children diving behind the sofa to hide from their terrifying enemies. It's down to the Doctor, with help from a trusty assistant and sonic screwdriver, to save the day.

The BBC series has been running since 1963, the world's longest running sci-fi show with more than 800 episodes.

But even the biggest fan won't have seen every episode. That's because at least 97 of them are lost.

Only a few years ago, that number was 137, so there's a chance more might yet be found – if Paul Vanezis has anything to do with it. He's a television producer and a keen film collector, who has tracked down dozens of lost Doctor Who shows. He believes more are out there, on forgotten rolls of film or in collectors' vaults.

But why are these 97 shows missing?

In the 1960s, the BBC didn't ever think that Doctor Who would run for so long. TV bosses were more interested in creating new episodes than keeping old ones. Back then, TV shows were stored on large rolls of videotape. This tape was expensive and space was tight, so programmes were wiped and the tapes reused.

The very first Doctor was portrayed by William Hartnell in 1963.

The Doctor battles Daleks, Weeping Angels, Cybermen, and more.

> YOU'LL NEVER COMPLAIN ABOUT REPEATS OF THESE SHOWS.

With so many films about cartoon cats being made, the studio wanted something different.

OSWALD THE LUCKY RABBIT

Mickey Mouse, the Disney icon, is famous the world over. His big, round ears are stamped on everything from T-shirts to lunch boxes. Those famous mouse ears could so easily have been rabbit ears, though, because before Mickey... there was Oswald.

In the 1920s, the animator Walt Disney made a deal with a film studio to make a series of short films based on a cartoon character. But who would this character be? They picked a name out of a hat, and Oswald the Lucky Rabbit was born.

Oswald was Disney's main cartoon character up until 1928.

The first film wasn't a great success. Oswald appeared old and serious. The animators went back to the drawing board and by the second film, the rabbit was younger, more mischievous, and fun. There was also a passing resemblance to a well known mouse who would appear a few years later...

For decades only 19 of Oswald's films could be tracked down. Then around 10 years ago, two more resurfaced, and a third in 2018. Now only a few remain lost.

In all, 26 Oswald films were made, by Disney and other animators. But Walt wanted a character that he could call his own, and so Mickey Mouse was born.

In 2022, Disney released a new Oswald film – *Oswald the Lucky Rabbit*, the first for more than 90 years! What's next? A Mickey and Oswald buddy movie?

ART

WRITERS' BLOCK

TWO VERY DIFFERENT WRITERS, BUT WITH ONE THING IN COMMON.

LOVE'S LABOUR'S WON

William Shakespeare was an English playwright of the 16th and 17th centuries, widely regarded as one of the greatest writers of the English language. He wrote around 38 plays including *Romeo and Juliet*, *Hamlet*, and *Macbeth*.

No copies of these plays exist in Shakespeare's hand – the closest thing we have is the *First Folio*, a collection of 36 of his plays from 1623.

In 1953, a specialist bookseller came across a book from 1637. As he leafed through it, some paper tucked into the pages slipped out. It was a handwritten note, dated 1603, containing a list of some of Shakespeare's plays, including *The Merchant of Venice*, *The Taming of the Shrew*, and *Love's Labour's Lost*. These plays are all well known today and have been performed on stage time and time again. However, also included on the list was another title: *Love's Labour's Won*.

No-one had ever heard of a Shakespeare play with this title, yet it was on the list. Was it a lost play? And if so, what was the plot? A sequel to *Love's Labour's Lost*? Who knows.

The First Folio was printed in 1623, after Shakespeare's death in 1616.

TERRY PRATCHETT'S HARD DRIVE

Terry Pratchett was a British fantasy author who has legions of fans, and who has sold more than 100 million books, in 43 languages.

Pratchett passed away in 2015 but he left a huge amount of unfinished writings, all stored on a computer hard drive. No doubt many fans hoped that these works might eventually be published. But Pratchett had other ideas.

He insisted that after his death, all his incomplete works should be destroyed. But Pratchett knew how to make a splash. He decided his hard drive would be crushed... by a steamroller.

And so, a couple of years after Pratchett's death, his assistant arrived at the Great Dorset Steam Fair, clutching the hard drive. A small crowd assembled as the drive was carefully positioned and they watched on in horror as the steamroller "Lord Jericho" rode over it. Surprisingly, the hard drive survived the experience better than expected, so to really guarantee nothing could be retrieved from it, the drive was placed in a stone crusher for good luck!

Pratchett is best known for his Discworld series, made up of 41 books.

Pratchett's hard drive was beyond saving, so his unfinished works will never be discovered.

On receiving a knighthood, Terry made his own sword, thinking every knight should have one!

STOLEN!
PERHAPS THESE PIECES STILL SURVIVE TO THIS DAY.

When something gets stolen, there's always a hope that it will one day show up. These fabulous pieces are lost to their original owners, so if you spot them, do the decent thing and call in the police!

SEEKING INFORMATION

The Isabella Stewart Gardner Museum theft

In the early hours of 18 March 1990, two police officers were shown into the Isabella Stewart Gardner Museum art gallery in Boston, Massachusetts.

However, those officers were in fact robbers. They handcuffed two guards, before cutting canvases out of a number of frames with a knife. They removed video tape of the raid filmed by security cameras, then calmly left the gallery with the canvasses.

Ransom

The Ghent Altarpiece

On 11 April 1934, a church warden opened up his church in the Belgian city of Ghent to discover part of a 500-year-old artwork was gone.

The piece was by the Flemish painter Jan van Eyck who painted Christ, Adam and Eve, and other biblical figures across 12 panels of wood. Over the years, sections had been stolen, hidden, and even almost destroyed by fire. Now two panels had vanished.

19 days after the theft, the Bishop received a ransom note for one panel, the Just Judges, demanding one million Belgian francs. The second panel was returned, seemingly as a goodwill gesture from the thief.

The authorities paid the ransom, but only 25,000 francs. The thief wasn't impressed, and the Judges remained missing.

Six weeks later, a former church worker was rushed to hospital. On his deathbed he admitted to knowing where the panel was. He uttered three words: "desk, key, closet" before he passed away. What did this mean? The police searched his home, but found no artwork.

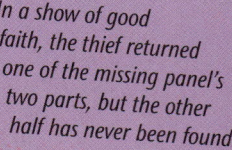

In a show of good faith, the thief returned one of the missing panel's two parts, but the other half has never been found.

$10 MILLION REWARD

Vermeer's The Concert and Degas's Leaving the Paddock were two of the stolen pieces.

They were inside for just 81 minutes.

13 paintings were stolen, including works by Vermeer, Rembrandt, and Degas, thought to be worth hundreds of millions of dollars today — the highest value museum raid ever. Despite a $10 million reward, the paintings are still missing.

The museum has a policy that nothing in the collection should be moved, taken, or added to, and so to this day the empty picture frames still hang on the gallery walls.

$100,000 REWARD OFFERED

The Davidoff-Morini Stradivarius violin

Stradivarius violins, made in 17th to 18th century Italy, are known for their craftmanship and extraordinary tone. Only around 650 of them still exist, and they sell for millions.

Austrian violinist Erica Morini was given a Stradivarius when she was 20, by her father. When she moved to the US, she kept it in a simple locked cupboard in her apartment.

When an elderly Morini was admitted to hospital in October 1995, someone entered her apartment with a key and stole her violin. No-one could bear to tell her it was stolen. A few days later she passed away, totally unaware of the theft.

The FBI interviewed all who had access to the apartment, but never charged anyone. 30 years after its disappearance, the violin is still lost.

Despite the theft being on the FBI's Top Ten Art Crimes list, nobody has ever discovered the whereabouts of Morini's Stradivarius.

ART

THE BAYEUX TAPESTRY

HOW DOES A BLOODY STORY STITCHED IN WOOL END?

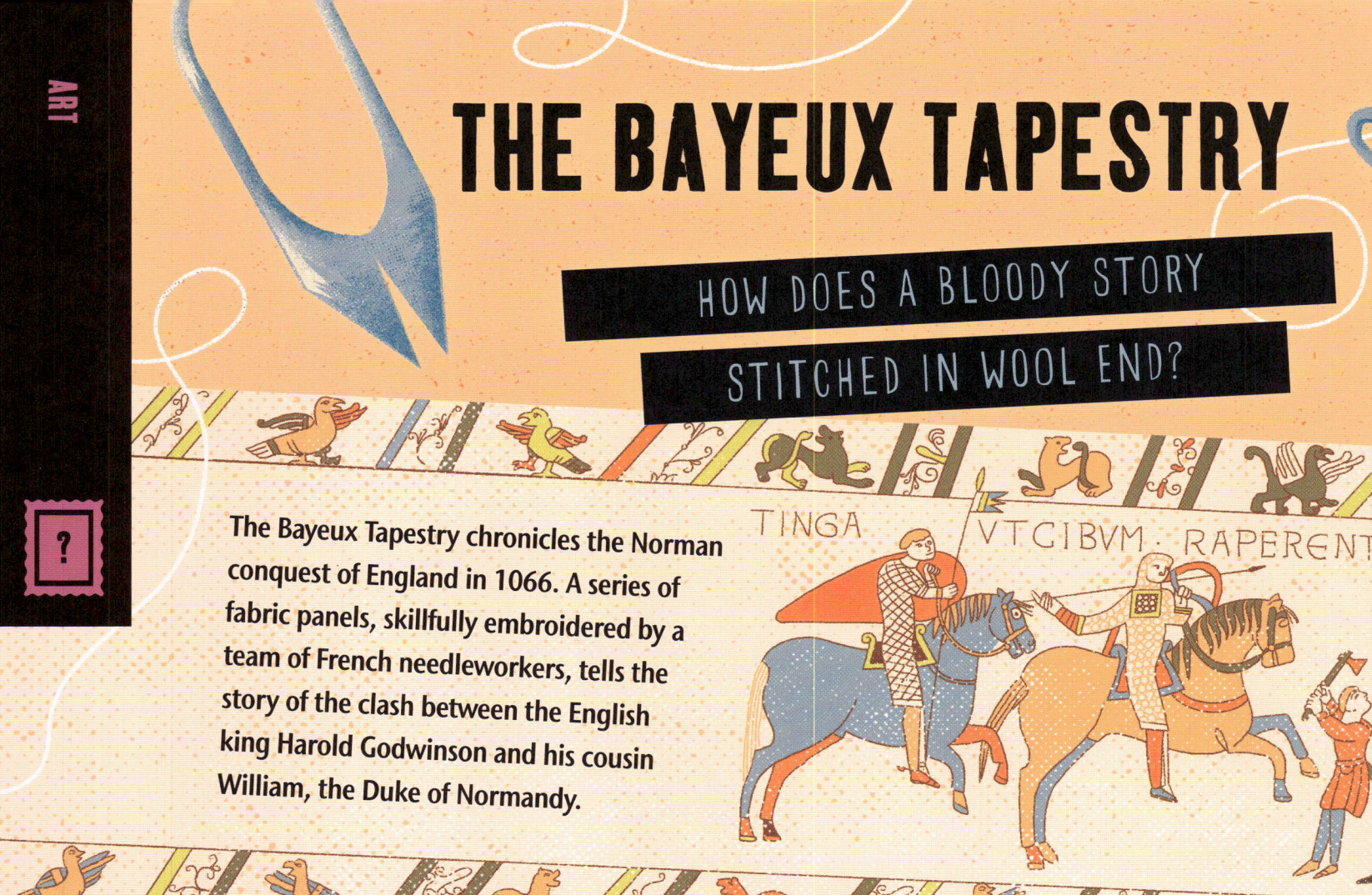

The Bayeux Tapestry chronicles the Norman conquest of England in 1066. A series of fabric panels, skillfully embroidered by a team of French needleworkers, tells the story of the clash between the English king Harold Godwinson and his cousin William, the Duke of Normandy.

A right royal battle

The Tapestry opens with Edward the Confessor, the recently deceased king of England, sending his brother-in-law, Harold, over to France. Edward had named his cousin William, Duke of Normandy, heir to his throne. But after delivering this message, Harold has himself crowned instead of William.

In September 1066, William leaves Normandy and crosses the English Channel with hundreds of ships. They land at Pevensey in Sussex, and make their way to Hastings to battle Harold for the crown.

Like a medieval graphic novel, all of this is carefully documented in 58 scenes of exquisite stitchwork across the 70 m (230 ft) tapestry, as is the final battle between William's Normans and Harold's Anglo-Saxons. Here, there are extraordinary details of intense fighting, ghastly injuries, cavalry charges, and regiments of archers firing volleys of arrows.

Eventually, there is a winner. Harold is struck in the eye by a Norman arrow and, as their leader falls, the Anglo-Saxons race from the battlefield, pursued by Normans on horseback.

An accidental cliffhanger

This is where the story ends though, because there is no final panel to the Tapestry, just a frayed edge. It's not known if there's just one scene missing or a whole collection. Thankfully, we know the history of the Norman invasion from other sources. William became king, with his sons following him to the crown. Most experts believe that a piece of tapestry around 3 m (10 ft) long has been lost. This might have illustrated William being crowned King of England on Christmas Day, 1066.

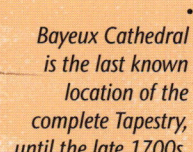

Bayeux Cathedral is the last known location of the complete Tapestry, until the late 1700s.

The Tapestry ends in a frayed edge where the final panel has been ripped away.

The Tapestry features 623 men, and only 3 women.

Revolution

It's believed that the Tapestry was held in Bayeux Cathedral until 1794, when France was in the midst of a revolution. Then the story gets a little murky. All we know is that by the time it was being publicly displayed as a work of art in the early 19th century in Bayeux, the end panels had already been lost.

Fabergé eggs

Fabergé eggs are fabulously ornate, jewel-encrusted ornaments, created by the Russian jeweller Carl Fabergé. Each egg, around 10-20 cm (4-7.8 in) tall, opens to contain a surprise.

The first egg was made for the Russian imperial family in the late 1800s. Tsar Alexander III gave it to his wife as an Easter present. He then ordered a new egg for his family each year, each unique and each worth millions.

At least 50 royal eggs were made but as the Russian Revolution hit, royal treasures were looted or sold off. Eggs occasionally pop up at auction today. In the US in the early 2000s, a man bought a pretty egg made of gold for around $14,000. It was actually the Third Imperial egg, worth $33 million!

Several of these exquisite eggs are still missing though, leading to the longest Easter egg hunt in history.

The Patiala necklace

This stunning necklace was created by the French jeweller Cartier in 1928, for the Maharaja of Patiala, in India. The necklace consisted of five chains laden with almost 3,000 diamonds. At its centre was the De Beers diamond, at the time the seventh-largest diamond in the world.

In 1946, the last Maharaja of Patiala was photographed wearing the necklace, the last photo ever taken of it. But as things changed in India and maharajas lost their land and livelihoods, the necklace vanished. No-one knows whether it was lost, stolen, or simply sold by a family desperate for money.

The finder of the Third Imperial egg initially bought it to sell for scrap metal, underestimating its value.

Yadavindra Singh, the last Maharaja of Patiala, was the final person to be photographed with the original necklace.

JEWELS AND JEWELLERY

YOU'D THINK IT WOULD BE DIFFICULT TO LOSE SOME OF THE MOST SPARKLING JEWELS IN HISTORY.

However, parts of the necklace have resurfaced. The De Beers diamond came up for auction in 1982. It sold for around £2.25 million. Then, in 1998 a Cartier expert spotted some of the necklace chains in a second-hand jewellery shop in London. Cartier bought them and used them as the starting point to restore the Patiala necklace, adding the extra chains and using synthetic diamonds to replace the missing ones.

In 2022, Cartier brand ambassador and YouTuber Emma Chamberlain wore part of the restored necklace to the annual Met Gala in New York.

The Three Brothers

The Three Brothers was a pendant made in the late 14th century. The "brothers" were three large balas rubies, cut into similar-sized rectangles. They clustered around a great blue diamond. Four pearls completed the piece.

It was made for the Duke of Burgundy in 1389. In 1504, one of the wealthiest men in history, Jakob Fugger, bought the jewel. But Henry VIII, King of England, wanted it for the English crown jewels. Henry died before he got his hands on it, but his son, Edward VI, completed the deal. Ten years later, Elizabeth I sported the Brothers in two famous portraits.

The piece was still part of the crown jewels 80 years later, during the reign of Charles I. When civil war broke out in England, the Brothers was sold to raise funds for armies. What happened to it then is unknown. Never seen in portraits again or written about in histories, it was lost, a victim of war.

Elizabeth I's favourite jewel is also carved onto her effigy on her tomb in Westminster Abbey.

Jewels, precious jewels. Well, if they were so precious, why weren't they better looked after? These jewels would all be worth eye-watering sums of money today, if only we knew where they were.

The Maya Codices

The Maya were a civilization that lived for thousands of years, across Central America. The civilization collapsed several centuries ago.

The Maya wrote on the bark of fig trees, folding pages in a fan shape to make books. We know this because of just four books, or codices, as researchers call them, that survive to this day. Each codex has a name: Dresden, Madrid, Paris, and Grolier.

For many years the Maya images and shapes were a code that couldn't be cracked, but once deciphered, they revealed details of the Maya religions and rituals. They are a fascinating glimpse into an ancient world, but there's still so much we don't know.

Of course, the Maya wrote more than four books. Sadly, many of these written works were destroyed by Spanish priests in the mid-16th century in an effort to erase the Maya religion, so almost all knowledge of the civilization has been lost.

The codices contain lists of numbers that the Maya used to predict lunar and solar events, such as the phases of the moon or eclipses.

ANCIENT WISDOM

WHETHER WRITINGS OR LANGUAGES, WE WOULD LOVE TO UNDERSTAND THE KNOWLEDGE OF THE ANCIENTS.

Words are a repository for knowledge, stored for future generations once written down. But if those writings go missing, or no-one can understand the language it's written in, that information is lost forever.

Rongorongo

On the island of Rapa Nui, also known as Easter Island, huge heads carved of stone stare impassively into the heart of the land. The origin of these moai statues is not the only mystery here.

A language, known as Rongorongo, was once used on the island. Today, no-one alive can read or translate any of the Rongorongo writing that remains. There isn't much to read — less than 30 pieces of text survive, carved into wood.

Perhaps the most bizarre thing about Rongorongo is the way it is written — in reverse "boustrophedon" style. Boustrophedon style has alternate lines going in opposite directions, so it is read from left to right, then right to left, and so on. And *reverse* boustrophedon? Well, you start from the bottom and work up, of course!

While the people of Rapa Nui do speak their own language, no-one knows how it relates to the written Rongorongo.

The Yongle Encyclopedia

Early in 15th century China, the third emperor of the Ming dynasty, Zhu Di, ordered that all knowledge be written down in one immense encyclopedia.

It was a bold demand! This great endeavour would cover every topic. Two thousand scholars wrote it over four years, and the finished work was huge: around 370 million Chinese characters long, almost 23,000 rolls of manuscript.

But despite three complete copies of the manuscript being made, today only around 800 rolls survive. The vast majority of the world's largest reference work has been lost, with fire and warfare most likely the cause.

For around 600 years, the Yongle was the most comprehensive encyclopedia ever written, until Wikipedia appeared.

KNOWLEDGE

LINCOLN'S LOST SPEECH

PERHAPS THE GREAT ORATOR'S GREATEST SPEECH... BUT WHAT DID HE SAY?

The 16th President of the United States, Abraham Lincoln, was a great orator – he was famous for delivering powerful speeches. Many of his speeches have been preserved in the history books.

His Gettysburg Address imagined a new United States of America, a place where all people were equal. At his Second Inaugural Address, he spoke about the birth of a new America after the horrors of the civil war. We know this because these brilliant speeches were recorded word-for-word.

The Gettysburg Address was one of Lincoln's speeches that did indeed get written down.

They are stirring speeches, and hearing Lincoln deliver them must have been even more inspiring. But there's a speech, perhaps the finest of his career, that no-one has a record of. The reason why? It was just too good! It's become known as Lincoln's Lost Speech.

Lincoln's campaign

Lincoln was a passionate anti-slavery campaigner. He wasn't alone in his determination to end slavery, but many were against him. In 1856, in Bloomington, Illinois, at a meeting called to persuade those against slavery to unite and fight as one, Lincoln gave an emotional speech about the evils of the trade.

More than 1,000 people had turned up to listen to the speeches that day. Lincoln never intended to speak, but late in the afternoon members of the crowd urged him on, and he stepped up onto the stage.

Too good to miss

Talking without notes, Lincoln gave an impassioned address against slavery, and how the only way to fight it was to unite under one banner: the Republican party.

Reporters began to scribble down Lincoln's words as he spoke. This was long before devices could record sound or pictures. As Lincoln's speeches were legendary, newspapers would want to print his address in full.

But after a few minutes, those same reporters found themselves so swept along by Lincoln's words that they put down their pens and just listened, transfixed.

So, while many talked of the brilliance of the speech, perhaps the greatest he had ever given, nobody wrote it down. While we know how extraordinary it was, we'll never really know what it was that Lincoln said.

KNOWLEDGE

LOST LIBRARIES

HUGE REPOSITORIES OF ANCIENT KNOWLEDGE, GONE FOREVER.

BAGHDAD HOUSE OF WISDOM

One of the world's largest public libraries, the Baghdad House of Wisdom, was established in the 8th century CE.

At the time, Baghdad was the capital of the Islamic world, an empire that stretched from Spain to modern-day Iran.

Works from great writers and philosophers such as Aristotle, Plato, Hippocrates, and Galen were collected for the library. Learning was deemed so important that when one Islamic leader, the caliphate al-Ma'mun, defeated his enemies, he demanded they provide texts and manuscripts for the growing library, instead of gold. This vast store of knowledge ushered in the Golden Age of Islam, which saw great leaps in science, engineering, and medicine, that spread across the world.

Sadly, this vast library was destroyed when the Mongols invaded Baghdad in 1258. So many books were thrown into the River Tigris, it was said that it ran black with ink.

Books were ripped apart and their leather covers used to make sandals by the Mongol army.

The library housed Arabic translations of texts about the science of medicine, and many other subjects.

LIBRARY OF ALEXANDRIA

Completed in the 4th century BCE, the Library of Alexandria is claimed to be the greatest library in antiquity.

Known as the Museion, it wasn't just somewhere to borrow or read books. It was a place of education, with more than 100 scholars researching, writing, lecturing, or translating documents.

The Library was said to hold more than half a million documents from across the world. There were works on science, religion, and mythology, along with essays about the study of knowledge itself.

Scholars were sent to foreign lands to hunt out new manuscripts, and any ships that entered Alexandria's harbour were required to hand over any books on board to the Library.

With so many rolls on the Library's shelves and oil lamps used for illumination, fire was a constant threat. In the 1st century BCE, the inevitable happened and some of the Library went up in smoke. Later years saw the destruction of libraries and temples by Christian rulers. By the 4th century CE, it was gone.

Papyrus is a kind of paper made from reeds, making the Library's contents vulnerable to fire.

KNOWLEDGE

THE ORIGINAL RENAISSANCE MAN

WHO KNOWS WHAT WE'VE LOST WITH LEONARDO'S MANUSCRIPTS?

Da Vinci mapped out designs for flying machines and other vehicles.

Born in 1452 in Tuscany, Italy, Leonardo da Vinci was an artist, scientist, biologist, mathematician, designer, engineer, and more.

While he's famous for paintings, he also kept notebooks in which he explored his many ideas. They contained designs for tanks, parachutes, and helicopters; detailed drawings of the anatomy of humans, and birds in flight; notes about his investigations into light, astronomy, geology, and even his work on solar power.

Organized chaos

Leonardo most likely worked on loose sheets of paper that were then bound into books. All of his drawings came with pages of notes, written in his famous "mirror writing" text. It's not known whether he wrote this way because he preferred it, or whether it was to keep his discoveries secret.

Scattered works

When he died, few seemed interested in Leonardo's works. He left his manuscripts to his assistant, Count Francesco Melzi, who passed them on to his son. Over time, as these books passed from person to person and the interest in Leonardo grew, they were cut up, reorganized, and turned into new books. Pages were given to royalty as gifts, others put in libraries. Some were stolen, sold on, or simply forgotten about in dusty collections.

Today, we don't really know how much of Leonardo's work is missing. Some experts think up to four-fifths of it may be lost. And of the pages that do remain, many have been so badly treated that we now can't read what they contain.

He designed weapons including the enormous wheeled crossbow.

New discoveries

But there is hope. Technology is allowing us to look in greater detail at what pages do remain. And incredibly, 500 years after his death, new pieces are still surfacing. Two notebooks turned up in a library in Spain in 1967. Knowing what we know about Leonardo, it's tantalizing to imagine what might be on pages still to find.

KNOWLEDGE

Liubo

Liubo was an ancient Chinese board game for two players. We know of it because game boards and playing pieces have been found in tombs, but how to play the game is still something of a mystery. Chinese archaeologists discovered a partial set of rules written across a large number of bamboo slips in 2019, but unless researchers can fully decipher them, the mystery around the gameplay will continue!

The game was popular from around 500 BCE to 500 CE. Each player had six pieces that travelled around a board marked with lines or routes. How those pieces moved, how far, and in what direction, we don't know, but it's thought players gambled on each of their turns. There were no dice. Instead, six sticks were tossed in the air, and how they fell determined how many moves a piece made. In fact, *liubo* means "six sticks" in Chinese.

Latrunculi

A two-player game popular throughout the Roman Empire, Latrunculi game boards, checkerboard style, have been found carved into temple floors.

Latrunculi was a military strategy game that may have had similarities to chess or draughts. What we know of the game comes from ancient writers, who reveal some of the rules and hint at the skill required to play.

Researchers believe there may have been 16 or 24 pieces per player, and each player took turns placing their counters on the board.

The aim of Liubo might be to travel the board, catching "fish" to eat.

Different parts of the Empire played Latrunculi on different sized boards.

LOST GAMES

WE ALL LOVE A BOARD GAME... BUT WHERE ARE THE RULES?

Once they were all in play, the counters could be moved forwards, backwards, or sideways. There were two special counters called the "dux" (one for each player) which could also leapfrog other pieces. The aim of the game was to capture all your opponent's pieces by surrounding an enemy piece with your own.

There were more complex rules that protected certain pieces and blocked parts of the board, but these can only be guessed at.

Mehen

Mehen was a game played by ancient Egyptians about 5,000 years ago, which makes it one of the oldest board games ever discovered!

The board resembled a coiled snake wrapped around the sun god, Ra. Pieces moved round and round along the snake's back, from the outer edge to the very centre, in a race to reach Ra. Instead of dice, marbles were used to indicate how far to move a piece, although how this happened is unclear.

Ancient Egyptian paintings show game pieces in the shape of lions and lionesses. Were these figures there to attack the players' counters as they made their way to the middle? Once caught, was a player sent back to the start of the board, like an ancient snakes and ladders game? We don't know.

Mehen was the name of a serpent god, hence the design of the board.

Humans have been playing board games for thousands of years. While some, like backgammon and draughts, have stood the test of time and are still played today, others have fallen out of favour – perhaps because we don't fully know the rules.

TREASURE!

THIS ISN'T A STORYBOOK PIRATE TREASURE MAP – IT'S THE REAL DEAL.

The planet's oceans are home to unimaginable riches. It's impossible to know all that has been lost to the waves across history: pirate galleons, ships transporting gold, and even those carrying wealthy passengers. Here's a taster of what treasure may lie below the surface.

SS Islander

The *SS Islander* was a passenger steam ship said to be carrying gold bullion worth over £5 million at the time it sank. In the early hours of 15 August 1901, it hit an iceberg. It quickly took on water and went down in less than 20 minutes. There have been a number of attempts to salvage the wreck, and in 1934 a section of the hull was raised and around £60,000 of gold nuggets found. In 2012, more gold was recovered, around £3.2 million worth. Despite the huge amount recovered, it's thought there's plenty more still down there.

The RMS Republic

In January 1909, the *RMS Republic* was steaming from New York to Europe with more than 700 people on board. Many of the passengers were very wealthy indeed – it's said that the ship carried over £2 million in gold alone. Navigating past Nantucket Island, they hit thick fog. The steamer continued, regularly sounding its whistle to warn others she was there. But this didn't stop another vessel, the *SS Florida*, ploughing into her. Although the wreck was found in 1981, the gold thought to be on board has yet to be recovered.

The Merchant Royal

This 635 tonne (700 ton) English galleon was making its way back from the New World in the mid-17th century when it stopped in Cadiz in Spain for repairs. There, the crew were asked to deliver a consignment of gold to Antwerp in Belgium. Unfortunately, before it reached its destination, the *Merchant Royal* sprang a leak, and in September 1641, it went down about 50 km (30 miles) off the coast of Britain.

MISSING

Cinco Chagas

In the 16th century, Portugal and England were at war. Somewhere off Faial Island, in the Azores in the Atlantic Ocean, the *Cinco Chagas*, a Portuguese carrack ship, was sunk. It was said to be loaded with 1,800 tonnes (2,000 tons) of treasure including 22 chests brimming with diamonds and rubies. By today's estimates, it was carrying a fortune worth billions, but the wreck lies in seas more than 1.6 km (1 mile) deep, making recovery of any treasure almost impossible.

The Flor de la Mar

When Portugal conquered the city of Malacca in the early 16th century, vast amounts of diamonds and gold were loaded onto ships heading back to Portugal, including the *Flor de la Mar*. However, it was a heavy ship to manoeuvre, and when it left port in November 1511, a storm drove it onto the coast of Sumatra. With so many riches on board, treasure hunters have spent fortunes attempting to track it down, but without success.

The Cahuenga Pass Treasure

Today the Cahuenga Pass is an eight-lane motorway on the US west coast. But in the 1860s, it was a simple dirt track close to the border of Mexico, where a revolution was underway against the emperor, Maximillian I.

Legend has it that revolutionaries collected gold, diamonds, and other jewels, and smuggled them into the US to trade them for guns. But the border area was teeming with Maximillian's supporters. So the revolutionaries headed up into the mountains to bury the jewels, and waited until the coast was clear.

A shepherd, Diego Moreno, spied them burying their loot. He dug it up then hid it again, burying it by an ash tree close to the Cahuenga Pass.

Moreno only revealed this story on his deathbed. Many set out to find that ash tree, but the treasure was believed to be cursed... Those who hunted for it all came to a sticky end.

Chief Two Moons fought at the Battle of the Little Bighorn.

Today the Hollywood Bowl sits where the ash tree was. Treasure hunters think the gold is somewhere under the carpark!

GOLD RUSH

ACROSS THE GOOD OL' US OF A, THERE'S TREASURE AT EVERY TURN.

Stories of lost treasure across the United States of America are rife. As the old saying goes, "there's gold in them thar hills"... if only you can find it!

Treasure at Little Bighorn

The Battle of the Little Bighorn in 1876 is famous as General Custer's Last Stand. Indigenous American peoples, including the Lakota and Cheyenne, defended their territory from the US Army. Neither Custer nor any of his men survived. The US soldiers carried gold and silver equivalent to more than half a million dollars today, which was claimed by the victors.

This might have been the end of the story, were it not for a trader called WP Moncure. He worked alongside the Cheyenne people and got to know Two Moons, an elderly chief who claimed to know where the treasure was buried. Two Moons died in 1917 but some years later an envelope with a message on it in Moncure's handwriting was discovered. Inside the envelope, it said, was the location of the treasure. It also stated that the envelope should not be opened until 1986.

So was Custer's treasure found? Frustratingly, the envelope was stolen before it got opened.

Dutch Schultz Treasure

Dutch Shultz, real name Arthur Flegenheimer, was born in New York in 1902. At 14 he joined a street gang, and from there went on to build a criminal empire worth $100 million.

Shultz was killed in the bathroom of the Palace Chop House restaurant.

Shultz was ruthless. It's said he was responsible for more than 130 deaths in just 10 years. The authorities were desperate to get him behind bars, but all that police attention was a problem for New York's other gangsters. Their solution? Get rid of Schultz. But what happened to his fortune?

Before he died, Shultz is said to have stuffed a strongbox with cash and diamonds and buried it somewhere in the Catskills Mountains. Some think he marked the site with an "X" on a nearby tree. Treasure seekers still search these mountains, but over time others have added their own "X"s on trees to throw rival hunters off the scent!

TREASURE

TUCKER'S CROSS

LOST, THEN FOUND, THEN LOST AGAIN.

In 1594, the Spanish galleon the *San Pedro* went down off the coast of Bermuda. It was part of the Spanish Treasure Fleet, a fleet of ships that took European goods to Spanish colonies in the Americas and brought back gold, silver, and other treasures to Spain. When the *San Pedro* went down, a host of extraordinary treasures went down with it.

Disappointing discovery

More than 350 years later, Teddy Tucker, out looking for shipwrecks on the dangerous reefs around Bermuda, thought he spotted a cannon muzzle poking out of the sand on the ocean floor. He dived down to have a closer look, armed with nothing more than a snorkel and flippers. He saw nothing to excite him though, so didn't explore any further.

The cross was inlaid with seven green emeralds, barely damaged by the water.

Lost once more

When the British monarch Queen Elizabeth visited the island in 1975, the cross was moved to the Bermuda Maritime Museum for a special exhibition. Tucker was to act as a guide and show the Queen the treasures he had found.

But when he inspected the cross ahead of the visit, he discovered a problem. The gold didn't seem as shiny as it once did. The emeralds had lost their sparkle. He picked up the cross, only to discover it wasn't his gold cross at all, but a piece of painted plastic. And the paint was still wet!

The police swung into action. Because the paint on the rogue cross was still wet, they believed the switch must have occured when the cross was moved from the aquarium. Suspects were questioned and leads were followed, but more than 50 years later, there is still no sign of the original cross.

Treasure at last

Four years passed before Tucker returned to the wreck. This time, he came across some fragments of porcelain and a few coins. Then, he spotted a small block of gold... Things had suddenly become very interesting.

Day after day, Tucker returned to the wreck, and soon he was pulling out gold bars, pearls, and other valuables, including a small, gold cross, about the size of the palm of his hand. It was a beautifully crafted piece.

Tucker was offered thousands of pounds for the cross from collectors around the world, but it ended up on display in the island's aquarium.

TREASURE

The Treasures of Lima

Cocos Island, 550 km (340 miles) southwest of Costa Rica, is said to be home to around $1 billion in buried treasure.

In the 17th century, the Spanish kept a treasure trove of gold, silver, and jewels plundered from other nations, in the Peruvian capital of Lima. By the 19th century, the Peruvians wanted to drive the Spanish out. To keep their treasure safe, the Spanish decided to ship it out of Lima.

A ship was hired and the treasures loaded on board, but the captain and his crew stole the booty and headed to Cocos Island... where he buried the fortune! He was arrested, but avoided being hanged after promising to lead the Spanish to the treasure. Unfortunately for the Spanish, once they arrived on Cocos, the captain escaped, disappearing into the jungle.

Buried gold at Loch Arkaig

In 1746, Bonnie Prince Charlie of Scotland hoped to reclaim the British throne from King George II. The French supported him, supplying gold to fund the rebellion. French ships made their way to the west coast of Scotland, carrying six caskets of gold coins, worth some £5 million today.

Sadly for the Scots, it didn't arrive in time to help in battle, and hundreds of Highlanders were slain by the British. Prince Charles escaped to France.

GOING FOR GOLD

HUNDREDS OF YEARS APART, BUT PEOPLE CAN'T RESIST THE POWER OF THE SHINY STUFF!

Only two weeks later did the French arrive with the gold. A clan chief buried the caskets close to Loch Arkaig, but then reburied them to keep one step ahead of the British. In the chaos of war, the stash got lost.

So where is it? An ancient letter may provide a clue. A witness claims to have seen the gold being buried and that he even helped himself to a bag of coins. The letter seemingly revealed the site of the gold — under a rock with a tree root springing from it, close to Arkaig. Is the letter genuine? Many believe it isn't. And of course no-one has yet found that rock... and certainly not the gold.

Nazi Treasure in Toplitz

In the 1940s the Nazis used Lake Toplitz in the Alps as a secret base for testing new weapons. But after the war, fake British bank notes started washing up on its shores. Investigators were curious – there were rumours that it was also where Hitler had hidden Nazi gold reserves, knowing he was going to lose the war.

A convoy of trucks had been seen arriving there shortly before the Nazi's defeat. Was this when the gold was hidden? US divers searched the lake, but it's a challenging place to explore. When one of the divers lost their lives, the hunt was abandoned.

The authorities have now banned diving in the lake but this hasn't stopped people having a go anyway, putting their lives in danger in the hope of finding Nazi gold.

The Nazis had likely intended to use the fake bank notes to sabotage the British economy.

Here's a tip. If you bury something valuable, make an accurate map! Three treasures are buried on a Pacific island, in the Scottish Highlands, and deep within a lake in the heart of Europe... But will they ever be seen again? It doesn't seem likely.

TREASURE

THE JULES RIMET TROPHY

NAZIS, SHEEPDOGS, AND THIEVES: THE TRIALS OF THE FOOTBALL WORLD CUP.

The first football World Cup competition for men was held in 1930 in Uruguay. Teams competed for a trophy officially called Victory. Later, the cup became known as the Jules Rimet Trophy, named after the President of FIFA, the world football governing body.

Uruguay won that first World Cup final. But the Victory trophy they won, a 10-sided, gold-plated cup held up by Nike, the Greek goddess of victory, has gone missing several times over its lifetime. It was last seen in 1983.

1938

First theft

Italy won the 1938 World Cup and the trophy went back to Rome. But with war looming, the President of the Italian Football Federation was worried the Nazis might steal it – so he hid it under his bed! The Nazis indeed came looking for the trophy, and even searched his apartment, but to no avail. It stayed under that bed until the competition resumed again in 1950.

Pickles' owner, David Corbett, was rewarded with £5,000, and Pickles received free dog food for a year.

1966

Final theft

Surprisingly, the cup was stolen yet again. One of the rules of the World Cup competition is that a nation can keep the cup if they win it three times. In 1970, Brazil achieved just that, and the trophy was theirs. It went on display in the Brazilian Football Confederation offices.

13 years later, thieves broke in and stole the trophy. A huge reward was offered, but the trophy was never found. Perhaps it was melted down, or sold on. Maybe it now lies in a collector's private museum, never to be seen by the public again.

1983

Second theft

16 years later, the trophy went missing again, this time in the host country of England. Ahead of the competition, the trophy went on display in London – but it was stolen.

It wasn't gone for good, though. It was found by Pickles the dog. Pickles wasn't a police dog or a trained sniffer dog, just a regular family pet being taken for a walk! Having a good sniff-around in the streets of south London, he discovered the trophy wrapped in newspaper and lying by a parked car. The England team went on to win the cup that year, but the thieves were never caught.

The current World Cup trophy was introduced in 1974, and has space to engrave 17 winning teams. A new trophy will be needed from the 2042 World Cup onwards.

SPORTING LOSSES

THROWN AWAY, OR JUST FORGOTTEN ABOUT... THERE ARE MANY WAYS TO END UP LOST.

THE BRUNSWICK-BALKE-COLLENDER CUP

Where is the Brunswick-Balke-Collender Cup? It's the biggest mystery in the history of the National Football League, the major league for American football in the US. The NFL started in 1920, and today 32 teams compete each year for the Super Bowl trophy.

The Akron Pros were the only NFL team to ever receive the Brunswick-Balke-Collender Cup.

That first year though, only 14 teams competed, and not for the Super Bowl trophy but for the Brunswick-Balke-Collender Cup.

Oddly, rather than the Cup going to the team that won the most games, it went to the team that were voted the best by the league's managers. That year, the Akron Pros from Ohio won the Cup.

However, after the Cup was awarded, it was never heard of, nor seen, ever again. All that remains of it is a solitary photo printed in the paper at the time.

MISSING

MUHAMMAD ALI'S OLYMPIC GOLD

Perhaps the greatest boxer of all time, Muhammad Ali was three-time undisputed heavyweight champion of the world and an Olympic gold medalist. Known for his quick wit and the famous "Ali shuffle", he taunted opponents, claiming he could "float like a butterfly and sting like a bee".

The Olympic gold was won in Rome in 1960, when Ali was just 18.

Ali, who had represented the US at the Olympics, was so furious about the discrimination he received from his fellow Americans, he hurled his medal into the Ohio River.

However, Ali did receive another Olympic medal. In 1996, after retiring from boxing and having worked as an ambassador for world peace, Ali lit the Olympic flame for the Atlanta Olympics and was awarded another Olympic gold, to replace the one he lost.

Following his Olympic success, Ali was so proud of his achievement that he wore his medal for 48 hours straight. But then, it disappeared. The truth of what happened to it is unclear, but one story is that Ali himself threw it away.

The champ had just returned from the Rome Olympics to Louisville in Kentucky, US. Still wearing his medal, he visited a restaurant to celebrate, but here staff refused to serve him because he was Black.

ROYAL TREASURES

DIAMONDS, KEEPSAKES, AND EVEN WHOLE THRONES AREN'T SAFE.

Across continents and throughout the centuries, trying to keep hold of precious treasures in the fog of war seems to have been fighting a losing battle.

The Koh-i-Noor diamond is the only surviving reminder of the magnificent Peacock Throne.

The Peacock Throne

The Mughal Empire, formed in the early 16th century, stretched from Afghanistan to Bangladesh. Shah Jahan, the fifth Mughal emperor, is famous for creating the stunning Taj Mahal, built in 1648, and 13 years earlier, the Peacock Throne.

Silver steps led up to a platform, on which stood a throne covered with rubies, pearls, and diamonds, including the huge Koh-i-Noor diamond.

Two carved peacocks (decorated with yet more jewels) flanked the throne, and shading the royal seat was a silk canopy atop 12 gold columns.

Of course, such a symbol became a coveted prize for any invader, and when Delhi was captured by Nadir Shah, the Shah of Persia, the throne was seized.

When Nadir Shah himself was assassinated and his palace looted, the Peacock Throne was lost to history.

The trail of the Florentine Diamond goes cold with Charles I of Austria.

Izabela's collection became the heart of Poland's first museum, the Czartoryski.

The Florentine Diamond

This infamous yellow diamond, the size of a walnut, has a cloudy history. In 1657 it was the biggest diamond in Europe and belonged to Ferdinando II de Medici, the Grand Duke of Tuscany.

The Medici family kept the gem until 1737, when it passed to the Holy Roman Emperor, Francis I. Fast forward 180 years, and the Emperor of Austria, Charles I, became the proud owner. As his empire fell apart during World War I, he was driven from his homeland, fleeing to Switzerland with the diamond. After that, its whereabouts are unknown.

Some claim the stone was stolen before it even reached Switzerland. Others say Charles hid it in a Swiss bank, or even had it recut into a smaller diamond. Whatever the truth, the Florentine is still lost.

The Royal Casket

Polish princess Izabela Czartoryska was an obsessive collector. Born in 1746, she loved literature, art, and history, and would travel across Europe snapping up decorative trinkets that appealed to her.

In a wooden chest she called the Royal Casket, she kept various precious relics from the Polish royal family: a gold watch, a bejeweled crucifix, a gold snuff box, a portrait of Queen Constance of Austria... In all, the Casket was said to contain 73 treasures.

War broke out between Russia and Poland in 1830 so Izabela, worried her treasures would be stolen, ordered the Casket out of Pulawy to Krakow. There it stayed until the Nazis invaded Poland in 1939, when it was moved again. In Sieniawa, it was hidden, bricked up behind a wall in a palace outbuilding. Sadly, it didn't survive the war. A palace insider revealed the hiding place to the Germans. Nothing was ever seen of it again.

CROWNS MISSING THEIR JEWELS

YOU'D THINK CROWN JEWELS AND ROYAL REGALIA WOULD BE BETTER LOOKED AFTER…

"Bad" King John is the villain in every Robin Hood tale.

The crown jewels of England

King John ruled England from 1199 until his death in 1216. He was not a popular king, and many wanted him off the throne.

In 1216, he was fighting a rebellion on the east coast of England. Pushed back by their enemies, the king and his men were trapped by the River Wash. They had no choice but to attempt a crossing, with horses, wagons, and more.

It was bad timing though, as an unexpected wave hit just as they entered the water. John travelled with his crown jewels, for safekeeping. But these, along with men and horses, were swept away.

The jewels included a gold crown, a belt of precious stones, and a collar set with diamonds. None were ever recovered.

Many have searched for these treasures, but nothing of note has been found. Since John's days, the Wash and its tributaries have been rerouted, so it's difficult to even know where to look!

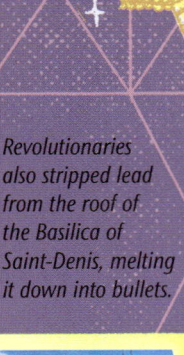

Revolutionaries also stripped lead from the roof of the Basilica of Saint-Denis, melting it down into bullets.

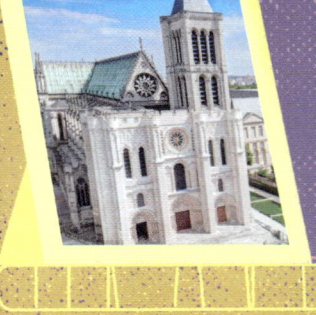

Surely if any jewels are safe, it's the crown jewels. After all, they're *the crown jewels!* But these stories prove that where there's a will, there's a way. Despite their significance, these crown jewels are all seemingly lost for good.

The Sceptre of Dagobert

This gold sceptre was a stunning piece, crafted for Dagobert I, King of the Franks, who ruled modern-day France and parts of Germany in the 7th century.

It was safely kept with other French crown jewels in the Basilica of Saint-Denis, a Parisian church and monastery. That is, until the French Revolution in the 18th century. Many expected the revolutionaries to loot the basilica, and so some treasures were hidden in the Louvre for safekeeping. Other valuables ended up at the National Library.

No-one is quite sure whether the sceptre was stolen from Saint-Denis or wound up elsewhere. But when the revolutionaries did arrive, they melted down any remaining gold treasures to cast them into coins… Did the sceptre suffer the same fate?

The Irish crown jewels

The Irish crown jewels were not linked to the Irish monarchy, but were a symbol of British power in the country at the time of the 18th century. They were kept under lock and key in a strongroom in Dublin Castle. That is, until 6th July 1907, when they were discovered to be missing.

The jewels had last been seen a month earlier but since then, a witness had seen the strongroom doors left open, and an intruder had been spotted, too! Scotland Yard offered a reward for any information on the whereabouts of the jewels, but with no luck. Some claimed they were buried in a graveyard outside of Dublin, but nothing was ever found.

There were many theories as to who was involved. Some insist political activists were to blame, angry about the British in Ireland. To this day, though, the Irish crown jewels remain lost.

Arthur Conan Doyle, author of the Sherlock Holmes detective stories, offered to help investigate.

ANCIENT CHINESE ARTEFACTS

To control the floods, Yu the Great dug channels for water to run off, and dredged rivers.

THE NINE TRIPOD CAULDRONS

Sometime during the third millenium BCE, China was hit by a series of great floods. Time and again, water swept away land and people. Crops were destroyed. Many died.

One man rose above others as a saviour. Yu the Great developed clever ways of controlling the floodwater. To the people, it appeared that the heavens had chosen Yu to lead, and the Xia Dynasty was born. China united behind him and to show thanks, the country's nine provinces each presented Yu with a gift of bronze, which Yu cast into nine cauldrons.

These cauldrons were the pinnacle of Chinese craft, true treasures symbolizing unity and a ruling from heaven. The cauldrons were passed from leader to leader as dynasties came and went, and began to represent the leader's power and authority to rule.

But where are they now? No-one knows. One legend has it that after the fall of the Zhou dynasty in 256 BCE, the cauldrons were lost in the Si River until Emperor Qin Shi Huang unified China in 221 BCE. Then the cauldrons magically reappeared. Ropes were used to haul the cauldrons out of the water, but at the last minute, a dragon appeared and bit through all the bindings. The cauldrons were lost forever.

A more believable outcome is that the vessels were melted down for coins or other bronze objects. But perhaps the cauldrons are still somewhere in the Si River, alongside a sleeping dragon...

LOSE THESE, AND YOU LOSE POWER AND AUTHORITY.

IMPERIAL SEAL OF THE REALM OF CHINA

Throughout history, seals (stamps used to print a character or design) have been used to mark ownership and prove identity on documents. An envelope sealed with the wax imprint of the king meant it carried the royal seal of approval — literally!

These seals were often made of wood, but in China, many were carved from precious stones such as jade, which was believed to reflect the inner beauty of the human body.

The Imperial Seal, also known as the Heirloom Seal of the Realm, was carved from jade in 221 BCE. It was then used by Chinese royalty on official documents for the next thousand years. Over time, it became a symbol for the power of the emperor. Whoever owned the Imperial Seal was, it was said, given authority by Heaven to rule. And so, when different provinces fought for control of China, the seal became a mark of status. Some believed the seal could choose its own path — the seal selected the country's leader.

The last dynasty to claim ownership of the seal was the Later Tang Dynasty. But when this line ended in 937 CE, the Imperial Seal was lost. How? Well, perhaps unsurprisingly, no-one really knows... If owning the seal gives you the god-given right to rule, you might keep quiet if you lose it!

In China, jade is a highly symbolic gemstone that signifies a bridge between the spiritual realm and the living, among other things.

The print from the Imperial Seal carried the authority of the emperor.

TREASURE

THE SECRET

HIDDEN GEMS

A REAL-LIFE TREASURE HUNT ACROSS THE US.

In 1982, Byron Preiss released *The Secret*, a book of 12 poems and illustrations that contained hidden clues for a real-life treasure hunt. Readers had to work out the locations of 12 small, ornate caskets that the author had buried in 12 secret sites all around the US.

Today the internet is full of theories about where the lost gems are hidden.

Each of those ceramic caskets contained a key. Sending the key back to the publisher would win the finder one of 12 precious gems including diamonds, rubies, emeralds, and pearls. These treasures were said to belong to some of the Fair Folk, goblins, fairies, leprechauns, and other magical creatures, who had all voyaged from their homes in Europe to start a new life in the United States. The book caused a real buzz on publication, as thousands across the world attempted to solve the puzzles.

Preiss has taken his nine secrets to the grave.

The first finds

It wasn't long before the first key was found. Just a year after publication, a casket was found in a park in Chicago. But it would be 21 years before the next one was found. A year after this second discovery, Byron Preiss passed away, taking the locations of the remaining keys to the grave. One treasure has since been found, in 2019, meaning that nine still remain... But the only way they will ever be found, is by solving the puzzles.

1983 Chicago

Three teenagers worked out the clues to find the first key in 1983 in Grant Park, Chicago. They dug in a number of locations around the park for six months before unearthing it, receiving a green emerald for their troubles. They set their sights on finding another key, but haven't had any success over the last 40 years.

2004 Cleveland

The next treasure was found in 2004, in the Greek Cultural Gardens in Cleveland, Ohio. The two lawyers who tracked the jar down captured themselves digging it up on video. They received an aquamarine gem for their efforts.

2019 Boston

Many people found the puzzles so difficult that they lost interest. Then, in 2018, the book featured on a TV show about mysteries. A new generation of treasure hunters got involved. Jason Krupat, a game designer, worked out one key was buried in Boston, under an old baseball pitch. His prize? A beautiful green peridot stone.

Jason Krupat's key was exchanged for a jewel worth about $1,000.

TECH AND INNOVATION

SWORDQUEST!

WHATEVER HAPPENED TO THE SWORD OF ULTIMATE SORCERY?

Atari was *the* games company back in the 1980s and their video game console, the Atari 2600, was a massive hit. Now fans could play their favourite arcade games at home. In 1982 they had a great idea to create a buzz around the release of a whole new game series.

Following the success of their first Dungeons and Dragons style game, *Adventure,* Atari followed up with *Swordquest,* a series of four games: *Earthworld, Fireworld, Waterworld* and *Airworld*.

What made *Swordquest* special was that there were real prizes up for grabs.

In the spirit of a fantasy adventure, members of the public would compete for a jewel-laden gold disc, a chalice encrusted with diamonds, a crown of gold, a gold box containing white jade, and a sword of gold and silver studded with jewels. Atari named these the Talisman of Penultimate Truth, the Chalice of Light, the Crown of Life, the Philosopher's Stone, and the Sword of Ultimate Sorcery.

Together these prizes were worth £110,000, around £365,000 today.

Live contests

To win, players needed to follow a trail of clues through each video game. If a competitor got all the clues right, they were through to the final – a live tournament game.

When *Earthworld* launched, half a million copies were sold, but only eight people were ultimately invited to compete for the Talisman of Penultimate Truth, by playing a new version of the game. Stephen Bell came out on top and took home the Talisman. Next came *Fireworld*, and 73 players got the clues correct. Eventually, these were whittled down to a single winner, Michael Rideout, who got his hands on the Chalice of Light.

But by the *Waterworld* launch, the computer games industry was changing and Atari was struggling. They had run out of money. *Airworld* was never even released.

Real-life quest

So what happened to the other prizes? The whereabouts of the Crown of Life, the Philosopher's Stone, and the Sword of Ultimate Sorcery are a mystery. They were never awarded to anyone.

Some wonder if the Atari boss might have kept them, but there's no proof. They could have been melted down, or sold to a private collector and guarded by a fierce dragon! The likelihood is, we will never know.

With the release of the Atari 2600 console, fans could play games such as Frogger, Pitfall, and Space Invaders at home.

TECH AND INNOVATION

ANCIENT TECHNOLOGY, GONE MISSING

DAMASCUS STEEL

Damascus steel was a type of steel that was used to make razor-sharp sword and dagger blades. Produced in Damascus (in modern-day Syria), the steel formed a blade that could cut a piece of falling silk in half.

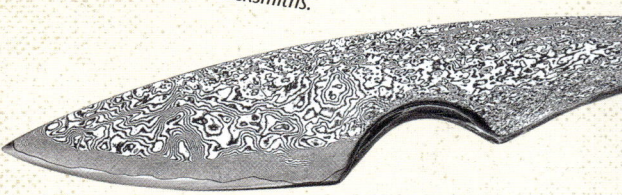

The pattern formed due to how the metal was forged – beaten with hammers while red-hot, by skilled blacksmiths.

Damascus steel blades were not only incredibly strong and sharp, but also beautiful, with a unique ripple pattern throughout the blade.

The steel was made for hundreds of years, from around 500 to 1750 CE. Then, in the late 18th century, blacksmiths appeared to lose the knack of making these exquisite blades. Any new knives dulled quickly, their sharp edges blunted in double-quick time. The knowledge of how to produce these brilliant blades appeared lost over a generation.

It turns out that it wasn't a lost skill, but a lost material. Steel is a mixture of iron and traces of carbon. Pure iron is too soft for a blade. Adding carbon makes the metal stronger, but too much and it can become brittle and prone to cracking, which isn't ideal mid-sword fight!

The steel used to make Damascus steel blades, which came from a specific place in India, had just the right amount of carbon, plus a few other elements, to produce a perfect blade. When the source of this iron dried up in the 18th century, and iron from other areas was used, the new blades were nowhere near as good.

WOULD IT BE POSSIBLE TO RECREATE THIS TECH?

ARCHIMEDES' HEAT RAY

Think ray guns are something from science fiction? Think again. The Greek doctor, writer, and philosopher, Galen, wrote of such a weapon being used more than 2,000 years ago.

He claimed a heat ray was used during the Siege of Syracuse, a city on the island of Sicily in the Mediterranean, off the coast of Italy. Syracuse was a Greek city, but around 214 BCE, some 60 Roman warships attacked it. Galen talks of an inventor, engineer, and mathematician, Archimedes, who created a series of weapons to defend the city from the Romans: giant catapults, a huge claw that could grab a ship and drag it under the waves, and of course, the heat ray.

If such a weapon existed all those years ago, how did it work? Well, no-one is really sure. The details have been lost over the centuries.

A series of curved mirrors could have been used to reflect the Sun's rays, concentrating them into a single beam powerful enough to set ships alight. It's easy to do this on a small scale. Focusing sunlight through a magnifying glass, for example, can generate a pinprick of light hot enough to burn a hole in paper. Imagine scaling that up with massive mirrors, and using the power of the hot Mediterranean sun.

Galen wrote about this heat ray 350 years after the attack. He never saw the weapon in action. So, did it exist? We can't say for certain.

Archimedes is also famously known for his work with levers and pulleys, and the invention of the Archimedes' screw device.

TECH AND INNOVATION

PROBES AND ORBITERS

KEEPING TRACK OF THINGS IN SPACE IS DIFFICULT, AS THESE STORIES PROVE!

It's not only ancient treasures that go missing. In the dark, vast expanse of space, it's very easy to lose things. There's even a toolbox orbiting somewhere around Earth, lost when it slipped out of the hand of an astronaut doing some DIY on the International Space Station!

Surveyor 2

Surveyor 2 was meant to touch down gently on the Moon and send photos back to Earth ahead of NASA's Apollo missions, but things didn't quite work out.

It blasted off from Florida on 20 September 1966. Days later, the spacecraft approached the Moon. As it slowly descended, its three legs were to unfold. Fitted with shock absorbers, they would ensure a gentle landing.

However, the craft never got to use its legs or any other clever equipment. A small thruster, used to adjust its direction, failed to fire. *Surveyor 2* went into an uncontrolled spin and crashed into the surface of the Moon at a speed of almost 9,650 kph (6,000 mph).

Surveyor 2 made its crash-landing on the Moon just three days after it was launched.

One of the Mars Climate Orbiter's objectives was to investigate how much water there might be on the Red Planet.

The Pioneer 10 was able to send back images of space objects such as Jupiter's largest moon, Ganymede.

During its 30 years of being tracked, the Pioneer 10 recorded several "firsts" – it was the first spacecraft to pass Jupiter.

Mars Climate Orbiter

In 1998, NASA launched their *Mars Climate Orbiter*, which was designed to send back information about the weather, atmospheric conditions, and climate on Mars.

It launched on 11 December 1998, and on 7 September 1999 sent back a photo of a distant Mars. As it approached, it was meant to enter into an orbit of Mars, around 226 km (140 miles) from the surface, where it would circle the planet, collecting data. However, the *Orbiter* ended up much closer to Mars than expected, where the atmosphere was denser. The craft couldn't cope with such dense air, stopped beaming data back to Earth, and was lost.

So how come the *Orbiter* flew so close to the planet? When scientists investigated the problem, they discovered there was a mix-up in units in the workings of the craft. Some of the computer software on the *Orbiter* measured thrusters in pound force-seconds, while other parts worked in newton-seconds. That's like getting metres and centimetres mixed up with feet and inches. Getting its sums wrong had major consequences!

Pioneer 10

Pioneer 10 launched from Florida in March 1972. Its mission was to head into the furthest reaches of the Solar System, sending information on its surroundings back to Earth. It passed the Moon just 12 hours after it was launched. A year later, it was approaching Jupiter, the fifth planet from the Sun.

Once there, *Pioneer 10* was able to beam back images of the gas giant, and researchers on Earth could see the planet up-close for the first time. With Jupiter ticked off, *Pioneer 10* then made its way further out into space, eventually crossing the orbit of Neptune in 1983.

By 1997 the probe was running so low on power it could only send faint pulses back to Earth. But still it kept going, out of our Solar System and into the dark reaches of space beyond.

When NASA finally lost communication with *Pioneer 10* in January 2003, it had become the most distant man-made object in the Universe. Who knows, it may be spotted by aliens in another Solar System one day...

NOT JUST ANY OLD ROCK

IT DOESN'T MATTER IF IT'S OUT-OF-THIS-WORLD, IT CAN STILL GET LOST!

How much would you pay for a lump of rock? Incredibly, some people are willing to part with millions for pebbles the size of a jellybean. Of course, these aren't just any old rocks... These are moonrocks.

Some moonrocks are almost 4.5 billion years old.

There have been six crewed landings on the Moon, the first in 1969, and at least 20 more uncrewed landings.

Across these trips, NASA has collected more than 350 kg (770 lb) of moonrock. Most of it is kept at the Johnson Space Centre in Houston, Texas. To ensure the Earth's atmosphere doesn't alter the rock in any way, it's stored in nitrogen gas and samples are only ever handled with gloves. By studying moonrock, scientists hope to understand more of the history of the Solar System and formation of the Moon.

However, not all of NASA's moonrock has ended up in the Johnson Space Centre.

The sample of moonrock was collected from the Taurus-Littrow Valley.

When Apollo 17 landed on the Moon in 1972, astronauts collected a piece of rock about 10 cm (4 in) across. It was broken into smaller pieces and Richard Nixon, US President at the time, gifted these nuggets of moonrock to leaders across all 50 US states and to heads of state around the world.

In all, around 270 of these "Goodwill Moonrocks" were handed out, each weighing around 1.1 g (0.04 oz) – that's about the weight of a jellybean! But if you thought rock this rare would be guarded carefully, you'd be wrong. Today, around 180 of these Goodwill Moonrocks have gone missing.

Tiny pieces of moonrock are said to have changed hands for up to £3.8 million. Even moondust will sell for £335,000, so it's no surprise that many Goodwill rocks have been sold or stolen, and that there is also a roaring trade in fake moonrock... which is just rock!

Hunting down the fraudsters

In 1998 a team of criminal investigators decided to clamp down on these scam sellers. They pretended to be moonrock collectors and placed an advert in a US newspaper. Some bogus rock sellers made contact and were then investigated by agents. While the team were offered fake moonrock, they also tracked down a real piece of the Moon, the Honduras Goodwill Moonrock, which, somehow, had found its way into a private collection.

Dumped

While some moonrock has been stolen or illegally sold to collectors, more has gone missing in other ways. One stone given to Ireland even ended up in landfill when the building it had been displayed in caught fire, and the burned remains were dumped. If you want to pick through piles of rubbish in the Finglas landfill in Dublin, there's £3.8 million waiting for you there!

The Goodwill Moonrocks were gifted to 135 heads of state around the world, by US President Nixon.

Each Goodwill Moonrock is about the weight of a jellybean.

87

TECH AND INNOVATION

Tybee island

On 5 February 1958, a US F-86 fighter jet on a training flight collided with a B-47 bomber over Tybee Island off the US state of Georgia. The pilot of the bomber looked to make an emergency landing but, worried that the bomb he was carrying might break loose as he hit the ground, he released it over water.

This was no ordinary bomb, though. This bomb was a Mark 15 hydrogen thermonuclear bomb – a bomb 190 times more powerful than the one that was dropped on Nagasaki at the end of the Second World War.

One hundred US Navy personnel were immediately drafted in to search for the device, but after two months of hunting, the search was called off. The bomb was never found.

Only nine countries in the world have nuclear weapons.

BOMBS AWAY

MISSING NUCLEAR BOMBS – SHOULD WE BE WORRIED?

There are a number of things you probably shouldn't lose: house keys, wallet or purse, or your favourite cuddly toy. But perhaps one of the worst things to lose is a nuclear bomb. Even so, a number have gone missing over the years, and they've still not been found.

Philippine Sea

On 5 December 1965, the USS Ticonderoga aircraft carrier was stationed in the Philippine Sea. For training purposes, the crew loaded a nuclear weapon onto one of their Skyhawk planes below deck, before bringing it up onto the flight deck.

The plan was for the plane to take off, circle the aircraft carrier, and come in to land. The device would then be safely removed.

However, once the plane and its nuclear cargo reached the flight deck, it began to roll to the side of the ship. Flightdeck crew signalled frantically for the pilot to engage his brakes, but he was too distracted. The plane tipped over the edge and into the sea.

A desperate search and rescue mission was launched for the pilot, but all that was ever recovered was his helmet. The plane, and the nuclear device, were also never found.

Greenland

In January 1968, a US B-52G bomber carrying four hydrogen bombs caught fire while flying over Greenland. Most of the crew members managed to eject safely before the plane crashed into sea ice. Explosives on board detonated, and nuclear material from the four nuclear bombs contaminated the area.

US airmen began a clean-up, collecting any traces of the plane wreckage or nuclear devices, however big or small. Any radioactive ice was also scooped up and taken away in sealed tanks. Upon studying the wreckage, all of the plane and its contents were accounted for... apart from the nuclear fuel component of one of the bombs. This still lies in the Greenland ice, somewhere.

TECH AND INNOVATION

MISSING BITCOIN

BE VERY CAREFUL ABOUT WHAT YOU THROW OUT!

Imagine taking a massive pile of money worth millions, and accidentally throwing it away. That's what one man claims to have experienced. The money is now, most likely, lost forever.

Back in 2013, thanks to an innocent mix up, a hard drive, part of a computer that stores information, ended up in a rubbish dump in Newport, Wales. That hard drive contained around 8,000 Bitcoin, a kind of cryptocurrency – a digital form of money that doesn't involve notes or coins and isn't controlled by banks.

Cryptocurrencies can be bought and sold on the internet for "ordinary" physical money like pounds or dollars, and over the years the value of Bitcoin has risen and fallen. The 8,000 lost Bitcoin were worth around £1 million back in 2013, but are now estimated to be worth more than £600 million. The lost hard drive wasn't noticed for a few weeks, but as Bitcoin increased in value, the search to get it back began.

The hard drive's owner did a bit of detective work to find out where his rubbish was dumped, and visited the managers of the site. By then, though, his bin bag had already been swamped by thousands of other bags, each full of rubbish. His hard drive was the size of a paperback book. The dump was bigger than 10 football pitches. Surely it was lost forever?

Could there be hope?

The managers explained that rubbish from a certain street always ended up at the same place on the dump. The drive's owner realized it was possible to pinpoint where his rubbish lay. Although there would be a lot to sift through, with the right number of people and enough time, the hard drive could be found. All he needed was access to the dump.

Making a plan

The council refused him access, saying it was too dangerous. Despite him offering them a share of his Bitcoin, he has yet to persuade them. However, he's pinned down the exact spot he's looking to dig, which includes around 100,000 tonnes (110,000 tons) of rubbish, and he believes 25 people could sort through it all in around nine months.

For now, the search has been paused, but who knows if the hard drive might be unearthed in the future! The problem is there's no guaranteeing it hasn't been damaged by more than 10 years in a rubbish dump. It may even have been recycled, or worse, crushed.

Although the missing hard drive is only small in size, it contains 8,000 digital Bitcoin.

Items from rubbish bins end up in huge landfill sites, along with piles of other things that people throw away.

GLOSSARY

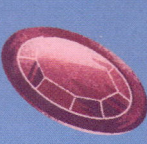

altarpiece
Artwork that is displayed behind the altar in a church

animator
Someone who makes animated cartoon shows or films

archaeologist
Someone who studies history through the examination of artefacts and discovery sites

artefact
Object of historical or cultural significance

aviator
Pilot of a plane

Bermuda Triangle
Region in the North Atlantic Ocean where aircraft and ships allegedly go missing

boustrophedon
Writing style in which text is written in opposite directions, alternating line by line (one line reading from left to right, followed by a line reading from right to left)

casket
Small box that holds valuable objects

circumnavigate
To travel all the way around something (for example, the world), ending where you started

codex
Ancient book that was handwritten

crown jewels
Jewellery worn by a king or queen during official ceremonies of the state

cryptocurrency
Digital form of money on the internet, which isn't controlled by banks

dynasty
Series of rulers of a country who all come from the same family

extinct
Species of animal or plant that no longer has any surviving members

fossil
Remains of an animal or plant, from prehistoric times, preserved in rock

French Revolution
Period of unrest in the late 1700s in France, resulting in the end of a ruling monarch in the country

hard drive
Part of a computer that stores data

iceni
Tribe ruled by Queen Boudicca, active in ancient Britain

looting
Stealing things during a time of unrest or chaos

maharaja
Ruler of a royal family in parts of India, before princely states were abolished in the 1900s

manuscript
Document historically written by hand, before printing was invented (today, a manuscript can be handwritten or typed)

moai
Huge stone figures found on the island of Rapa Nui

monarchy
Country that is ruled by a monarch (a king, queen, emperor, or empress)

motorcade
Procession of vehices travelling slowly while carrying important people, often as part of a parade or ceremony

NASA
National Aeronautics and Space Administration, an American goverment organization for space exploration

orator
Somebody who is particularly skilled at performing speeches

orbiter
Spacecraft or satellite designed to orbit (travel around) a planet or moon but not land on it

pharaoh
A king of ancient Egypt

pirate
Sailor who attacks or steals from other ships

privateer
Commander or crew member of an armed ship, privately hired to attack or capture enemy ships

Richter scale
Scientific scale used to measure the strength of earthquakes

Roman Empire
Ancient empire that spread from Rome to encompass various territories across Europe, North Africa, and Asia

sarcophagus
Decorative container, similar to a coffin, used to hold a person's body

sceptre
Decorative, ornamental staff carried by royalty during ceremonies, as a symbol of power

tsar
Historical title for Russian monarchs between the years of 1547 and 1917

tsunami
Large and often destructive tidal wave, usually triggered by an earthquake

Tutankhamun
Ancient king of Egypt from 1361 to 1352 BCE

INDEX

A

Alexander the Great 18-19
Alexandria 19, 21
Ali, Muhammad 71
amber 24, 25
Apollo 17 86
Archimedes 83
Atari 80

B

Babylon 19, 22
Baghdad House of Wisdom 54
Barbary lion 13
Battle of Hastings 46
Battle of the Little Bighorn 63
Battle of Watling Street 21
Bayeux Tapestry 46-47
BBC 40
Bermuda Triangle 36, 37
Bitcoin 90, 91
Bonaparte, Napoleon 20
Boudicca 21, 34
Brunswick-Balke-Collender Cup 70

C

Caesar, Julius 19, 35
Caroll A. Deering 37
Cartier 48, 49
Celtic tribes 34
Charles I of Austria 73
Cheyenne peoples 63

Cinco Chagas 61
Cleopatra 20-21
Colossus of Rhodes 23
Cooper, D. B. 28-29
copper scroll 10, 11
Count Francesco Melzi 57
Cromwell, Oliver 33
crown jewels of England 49, 74
Cybermen 40
Czartoryska, Izabela 73

D

da Vinci, Leonardo 56-57
Dagobert I 75
Daleks 40
Damascus steel 82
Davidoff-Morini Stradivarius violin 45
De Beers diamond 48, 49
de Medici, Ferdinand II 73
Discworld series 43
Disney 41
Doctor Who 40
dodo 12

E

Earhart, Amelia 9
Edward the Confessor 46
Egyptian mummy 32
Emperor Qin Shi Huang 76
English Civil War 33

F

Fabergé eggs 48
FBI 29, 31, 45
First Australians 27
First Folio 42
Florentine Diamond 73
French Revolution 32, 47, 75

G

Galen 54, 83
General Custer's Last Stand 63
Gettysburg Address 52
Ghent Altarpiece 44
Godwinson, Harold 46
Goodwill Moonrocks 87
Great Pyramid, Giza 22
Great Tetrapylon 27

H

Hanging Gardens of Babylon 22
Henry VIII 49
Hillary, Edmund 8
Hitler, Adolf 24, 38, 67
Homo erectus 6
hydrogen bombs 88

I

Iceni 21, 34
Imperial Seal 77
Irvine, Andrew "Sandy" 8
Isabella Stewart Gardner Museum 45

J

jade 77
Johnson Space Centre 86
Jules Rimet trophy 68-69
Juukan Gorge 27

K

Kennedy, John F 30-31
Khan, Genghis 18
King John of England 74
Koh-i-Noor diamond 72

L

Lake Toplitz 67
Lakota peoples 63
Latrunculi 58, 59
Library of Alexandria 55
Lighthouse of Alexandria 22
Lincoln, Abraham 52, 53
Liubo 58
Loch Arkaig 66, 67
Louis XIV 32
Love's Labour's Won 42

M

Maharaja of Patiala 48
Mallory, George 8
marble faun 38
Mark Antony 20
Mars Climate Orbiter 85
Mausoleum of Halicarnassus 22

Maximillian I 62
Maya civilization 50
Maya codices 50
Mehen 59
Menkaure 19
Michelangelo 38
Mickey Mouse 41
Ming dynasty 51
Moai statues 51
Monuments Men 39
moonrocks 86, 87
Morgan, Henry 17
Mount Everest 8
Mughal Empire 72

N

NASA 84, 85, 86
Nazis 24, 25, 38, 39, 67, 68
Nefertiti 20
Niger National Museum 15
Nixon, Richard 86, 87
Norgay, Tenzing 8
Norman conquest 46

O

Olympia temple 23
Oswald the Lucky Rabbit 41
Oswald, Lee Harvey 31

P

Palmyra 27
Patiala necklace 48, 49
Pau, Alexandre 32
Peacock Throne 72
Peking Man 6-7
Peter the Great 24

Phideas 23
Pinikura peoples 27
Pioneer 10, 85
pirates 16, 17, 37
Port Royal, Jamaica 16-17
Portrait of a Man 38
Pratchett, Terry 43
Preiss, Byron 78, 79
Prometheus 14
Ptolomy 19
Puerto Rico Trench 36
Puutu Kunti Kuruma peoples 27
pyramids of Giza 19

R

Rapa Nui (Easter Island) 51
Rembrandt 45
RMS Republic 60
Rodin, Auguste 39
Roman Empire 13, 58
Roman legions 34-35
Roman Ninth Legion 34-35
Rongorongo 51
Russian Revolution 48

S

San Pedro 64
Sappho 39
sarcophagus of Menkare 19
sceptre of Dagobert 75
Schlüter, Andrea 24
Seven Wonders of the World 22-23
Shah, Nadir 72
Shakespeare, William 33, 42
Shultz, Dutch 63

Singh, Yadavindra 48
Spanish Treasure Fleet 64
St Mark's Basilica 18
Statue of Zeus 23
Surveyor 2 84
Swordquest 80, 81
Sycamore Gap tree 15

T

Taj Mahal 72
Tang Dynasty 77
Taposiris Magna 20, 21
Temple of Artemis 22
The Painter on His Way to Work 39
The Secret 78
The Three Brothers 49
Theodosius 23
Third Imperial Egg 48
treasures of Lima 66
Tree of Ténéré 15
Tsar Alexander III 48
Tucker, Teddy 64, 65
Tutankhamun 20

U, V

Ubar 26
USS Cyclops 36
van Eyck, Jan 44
Van Gogh, Vincent 39
Vanezis, Paul 40
Vyse, Howard 19

W

Walt Disney 41
Wheeler Peak, New Mexico 14
William, Duke of Normandy 46, 47
World Cup trophy 68, 69

X, Y, Z

Xia Dynasty 76
Yongle encyclopedia 51
Yu the Great 76
Zhou Dynasty 76
Zhu Di 51

ACKNOWLEDGEMENTS

DK would like to thank Rituraj Singh and Samrajkumar S for picture research help; Lois Ware for proofreading; and Claire Sipi for the index.

The publisher would like to thank the following for their kind permission to reproduce their photographs:

(Key: a-above; b-below/bottom; c-centre; f-far; l-left; r-right; t-top)

6 Getty Images: The Chronicle Collection / Carl Mydans (cl). **7 Science Photo Library:** Pascal Goetgheluck (tr). **8 Getty Images:** Royal Geographical Society (tc, cr). **9 Getty Images:** Bettmann (bl). **10 Alamy Stock Photo:** Über Bilder (cl). **11 Alamy Stock Photo:** ART Collection (bc). **12 Science Photo Library:** Natural History Museum, London (crb). **13 Getty Images:** LightRocket / Frank Bienewald (cr). **14 Joshua Winkler:** (cr). **15 Alamy Stock Photo:** Arterra Picture Library / Van Der Meer Marica (cr); PA Images / Owen Humphreys (cla). **17 Texas A&M University:** Dr. Donny Hamilton (cr). **18 Alamy Stock Photo:** Mauritius Images GmbH / Dennis Schmelz (bl). **Getty Images:** Jakub Chrzanowski (br). **19 Alamy Stock Photo:** Joana Kruse (bc). **20 Alamy Stock Photo:** Mark Davidson (cr). **Getty Images:** Subjects / Robertharding / Richard Maschmeyer (clb). **21 Alamy Stock Photo:** Travelib History (cr). **23 Alamy Stock Photo:** Album (cra). **26 Dreamstime.com:** Christoph Lischetzki (cr). **27 Dreamstime.com:** Monikamonia (tr). **28 Alamy Stock Photo:** Everett Collection (cra). **29 Alamy Stock Photo:** American Photo Archive (crb). **Getty Images:** Bettmann (br). **30 Alamy Stock Photo:** World History Archive (tr). **31 Alamy Stock Photo:** Alpha Historica (tl). **Dreamstime.com:** Qiwoman01 (cl). **32 Alamy Stock Photo:** B Christopher (cb). **33 Alamy Stock Photo:** Adam Eastland (cb); Penta Springs Limited / Artokoloro (tc). **34 Alamy Stock Photo:** De Rocker (bl). **35 © York Museums and Gallery Trust 2025:** (bc). **36 Alamy Stock Photo:** U.S. Department of Defense Archive (cra). **37 Getty Images:** Bettmann (c). **39 Alamy Stock Photo:** Album (cl); History and Art Collection (crb). **40 BBC Photo sales:** (crb). **41 Alamy Stock Photo:** Bill Waterson (c). **42 Alamy Stock Photo:** Shawshots (bl). **43 AFP:** Richard Henry (br). **Getty Images:** Peter Macdiarmid (cr). **44 Bridgeman Images:** Art in Flanders (bc). **44-45 Getty Images:** Boston Globe (ca). **45 Alamy Stock Photo:** Associated Press (bl). **47 Alamy Stock Photo:** Peter Cavanagh (bl). **Getty Images / iStock:** Guy-Ozenne (tr). **48 Alamy Stock Photo:** Album (cl). **Shutterstock.com:** British India Collection (cr). **49 Alamy Stock Photo:** The Picture Art Collection (cr). **Getty Images:** AFP / Shaun Curry (cl). **50 Alamy Stock Photo:** Album (cr). **51 Alamy Stock Photo:** Piemags (bc). **Getty Images:** De Agostini / Dea / G. Nimatallah (cla). **52 Alamy Stock Photo:** CBW (c). **54 Alamy Stock Photo:** Realy Easy Star (br). **56 Alamy Stock Photo:** Incamerastock / ICP (tr). **57 Alamy Stock Photo:** Historical Images Archive (cla); Incamerastock / ICP (bl). **58 Alamy Stock Photo:** Penta Springs Limited / Artokoloro (c). **58-59 Alamy Stock Photo:** FOST (c). **59 Alamy Stock Photo:** Alain Guilleux (c); MET / BOT (cb). **60 Alamy Stock Photo:** Associated Press (crb). **62 Alamy Stock Photo:** GoHollywood (clb); Imago History Collection (tr). **63 Getty Images:** Archive Photos / Hulton Archive (crb). **65 Alamy Stock Photo:** Joel Zatz (tl). **67 Alamy Stock Photo:** Keystone Press / Keystone Pictures USA (cr). **68 Getty Images:** Mary Turner (tr). **69 Alamy Stock Photo:** Keystone Press / Keystone Pictures USA (tl). **Getty Images:** AFP / Claudio Santana (br). **70 Alamy Stock Photo:** FLC 2021A (cr). **71 Getty Images:** Hulton Archive / Central Press (cl). **72 Alamy Stock Photo:** The Natural History Museum, London (cb). **73 Alamy Stock Photo:** Album (tr); Süddeutsche Zeitung Photo / Scherl (tl). **74 Alamy Stock Photo:** Chronicle (c); Hemis / Chicurel Arnaud (br). **75 Alamy Stock Photo:** Archive Pics (br). **76 Alamy Stock Photo:** Universal Art Archive (tc). **77 Dreamstime.com:** Vvoevale (tr). **78 Getty Images:** Archive Photos / Karjean Levine (bc). **79 Getty Images:** Boston Globe (bl). **81 Alamy Stock Photo:** Arcadelmages (ca); Photology1971 (br). **82-83 Dreamstime.com:** Maxim Stukonozhenko (ca). **83 Alamy Stock Photo:** AF Fotografie (bc). **85 NASA:** (ca). **86 Science Photo Library:** NASA (bc). **87 Alamy Stock Photo:** The Natural History Museum, London (cr). **90 Dreamstime.com:** Asafta (bl, bc). **91 Dreamstime.com:** Dragan Andrii (bc); Asafta (bl). **Getty Images:** Matthew Horwood (br)

Cover images: *Front:* **Alamy Stock Photo:** Album tl, Travelib History cra; **Dreamstime.com:** Asafta crb, Igor Stramyk bl; **Getty Images:** AFP / Shaun Curry cl; **Getty Images / iStock:** Ugurhan Betin br; *Back:* **Alamy Stock Photo:** Mauritius Images GmbH / Dennis Schmelz bl, The Natural History Museum, London cra; **Dreamstime.com:** Dragan Andrii tr, Vvoevale tc

From the author:

I'd like to thank George, Eddie, and Ben for inspiring the idea, Jo for her patience and support, Daniela for providing the most perfect imagery to this collection of stories, and to Abi and James at DK for making the whole process so collaborative and enjoyable.

From the illustrator:

Remember, history is not a thing of the past. It writes itself every day with the stories of everyone in the world. I hope this book makes you an explorer, and that you find beauty in discovering stories different from yours. To Juan, who said, "Life is infinite".